MW01409716

Black Pearls

# BLACK PEARLS

*Improvisations on a Lost Year*

SASCHA FEINSTEIN

Eastern Washington University Press

Copyright © 2008 Eastern Washington University Press
All rights reserved.

14  13  12  11  10  09  08    5  4  3  2  1

Cover photograph: Sascha Feinstein and his mother, ca. 1967.

Cover and interior design by Liz Lester

*Library of Congress Cataloging-in-Publication Data*

Feinstein, Sascha, 1963–
    Black pearls : improvisations on a lost year /
  Sascha Feinstein.
        p.   cm.
    ISBN 978-1-59766-047-1 (alk. paper)
    1. Feinstein, Sascha, 1963–  I. Title.
    PS3556.E435Z46   2008
    811'.54—dc22
    [B]
                            2008028388

The paper used in this publication meets the requirements of
ANSI/NISO Z39.48-1992 (Permanence of Paper).

Eastern Washington University Press
Spokane and Cheney

*for Anita's grandchildren*
*Kiran & Divia*

In the end, those who were carried off early no
		longer need us:
they are weaned from earth's sorrows and joys,
		as gently as children
outgrow the soft breasts of their mothers. But we,
		who do need
such great mysteries, we for whom grief is so often
the source of our spirit's growth—: could we exist
		without *them*?

					—Rainer Maria Rilke


The memory of things gone is important to a jazz musician. I remember I once wrote a sixty-four-bar piece about a memory of when I was a little boy in bed and heard a man whistling on the street outside, his footsteps echoing away.

					—*Duke Ellington*

# CONTENTS

| | |
|---|---|
| Rearview Mirror | *3* |
| Spells | *15* |
| The Pheasant's Reflection | *27* |
| The Wide Hands of Charles Mingus | *37* |
| Blouse Catching Smoke | *49* |
| Where We Sleep | *59* |
| Thelonious Maximus | *71* |
| Black Pearls | *81* |
| Mormor | *93* |
| Before | *103* |
| Transcriptions | *111* |
| Lost Works | *121* |
| Fire : Ceremony | *129* |
| On Angels and Demons | *139* |
| Emerald Hummingbird | *149* |
| In Honor of the Sacred Heart | *159* |
| *Acknowledgments* | *169* |

Black Pearls

# Rearview Mirror

What were my last words to my mother? I had never considered the question and had forgotten how she slept for a day and a half before she died. Up until recently, in fact, I considered my junior year in high school to be "the lost year," a landmark period with a few markers and no land. I knew it began in early September 1979 and ended mid-April 1980—the unexpected diagnosis of my mother's cancer, and then her death—but I couldn't piece the narrative together, nor did I ever know what memories would emerge, or when. Dramatic events. Evasive fragments. Sometimes, just color or sound.

 I didn't write much about the experience during the year itself or the next, but those minimal fragments of memory fueled my poems and stories in college, and then in graduate school—so much so that, ironically, I began to feel trapped by experiences I could barely conjure. I didn't *want* to write another poem about my mother's cancer and kept reprimanding myself: "*Enough*. Get on with your life." Dwelling on loss seemed utterly self-centered—because it is, if loss becomes one's only focus. I assumed I had recollected everything meant to return to my consciousness and that it didn't matter if I could not place a single event chronologically. In essence, I accepted the mind's erasure.

Then, twenty years later, I found myself able to revisit that lost year and began to connect events. At first, I thought my greatest triumph would be to create a linear timeline: the date of the initial diagnosis; the number of weeks we lived thinking the cancer might be microscopic and therefore killed with radiation; the word *terminal*; the reality of that word; the passing; the immediate aftermath. I wanted to place individual visitors, and groups of visitors, and particular moments that I recalled for both spectacular and mundane reasons. I thought control meant constructing a calendar, but now that the dates have been slotted into place (more or less), the nature of this return seems so much more expansive, as if challenging time itself.

The trigger for this dramatic transition in sensibility and consciousness arrived in 1999 when I returned to New York to aid my father, who had undergone an aortic valve replacement. The poor staffing at Mount Sinai kept me in the hospital for long hours, and I felt an oddly parental obligation to oversee his treatment. That's not to say my father welcomed my help; disgusted by his vulnerability, he scowled at my attention. But one morning I brought my electric razor to shave him, and he smiled broadly—the first look of true happiness after the operation. I remember pulling up a chair as he puffed his cheeks, and while the razor hummed and buzzed, I realized how little I had done for my mother during her illness. I brought her things, of course, and sometimes I would wash her feet, but every act that suggested the duties of a nurse emphasized a truth I so wanted to deny. True, being with my father wasn't exactly parallel: it's one thing to preserve the dignity of the living, and quite another to comfort the dying. But as his soft skin emerged, I found myself unable to dismiss comparisons, and it seemed almost ceremonial when I tapped the razor onto an old newspaper and folded the dustlike hair into the *Times*.

Two weeks later, after he'd been brought home and seemed to be recovering well, I felt comfortable leaving and exited at 96th onto the West Side Highway on my way to central Pennsylvania. I'd grooved this route between my childhood home and my new one, so I didn't feel daunted by the substantial traffic and the lousy weather. Inside the car, I could hear only two things: a Charlie Parker tribute on WKCR, and a thunderous rain that consumed the city. *Parker and weather reports,* I thought. *Perfect guides home.*

Most people know of Charlie Parker's astonishing music and his wildly self-destructive life. Rarely did his excessive behavior destroy his artistry, but at least two infamous recordings prove that even Parker's stamina could not sustain the intensity of depression, and they remain some of the saddest recordings I own. The first almost-unlistenable session is from late July 1946. Scholars call it the "Lover Man" session because on that ballad, Parker loses command and, in a matter of hours, is taken to Camarillo, a mental institution where he will remain for six months.

Phil Schaap, the host of WKCR and an encyclopedic jazz scholar, was introducing the second breakdown: music from a Carnegie Hall concert on September 25, 1954, when Parker couldn't quite finish "My Funny Valentine." It's his daughter's unexpected death, Schaap announces several times, that precedes and shapes these recordings of heartbreak. I knew enough of that history to imagine Parker on the West Coast, hearing of Pree's death and sending his wife four bewildered and disjointed telegrams. Hard to absorb, also, the fact that Parker dies just a few months later, on March 12, 1955. He was thirty-four. I'd already outlived him.

Outside, the rain fell with such a fury that I thought it might be hail. Cars began to hydroplane. Some pulled to the berm. I could see the fogged outline of the George Washington Bridge and pressed on. Someone on the radio announced that this was record rain, that people should stay inside because sections of the highway had been washed out. That's when the exits began to close.

At first, the closings hardly registered because they started at the southern end of the highway, but when they closed 96th Street, I knew the storm had manhandled the city. Then the exits shut down closer to the time when I passed them, and I began to imagine the world disappearing behind my tires. Defrosting the windshield and mirrors did not clear the opaque rain and fog, and I kept wiping away nothing but my own hand. Behind me: grey and gray. I felt like someone fleeing from a tornado, or like a character in a science fiction movie who's chased by a consuming time warp.

Parker's music and Parker's life. My father's illness and recovery. The whole highway vanishing in my rearview mirror. When I crossed from Jersey into a much-sunnier Delaware Water Gap, all three fused into memory's prism, and I fell back twenty years to Friday, March 14, 1980. My mother had a month to live. I was seventeen by a day. And the West End Jazz Café was honoring the twenty-fifth anniversary of Charlie Parker's death.

Now defunct, the West End used to be located on 113th and Broadway, and throughout the 1970s and early '80s it mainly featured outstanding sidemen who never attained the fame of their leaders but who almost always provided an evening of lasting music. Many knew the club as the hangout for Columbia students because of its proximity to the university and because it sold reasonable grad school grub. I listened to many wonderful piano players, including old Sammy Price from Kansas City, and Ram Ramirez, who composed "Lover Man." Ramirez once spent an evening complaining—even from the stand!—that he had to suffer through the gig instead of attending a huge party hosted by Ruth Ellington, Duke's daughter; another night, he backed a student vocalist from the Eastman School of Music who sat in with his trio because, she said, "Lover Man" was her signature tune. (She was dreadful.) I heard many other pianists, too many to name, and liked almost all of them, even though the piano itself wasn't terribly good. As Lee Konitz said to the crowd one evening, "That's the great Dick Katz on piano . . . I'm calling it a piano; you know what it is."

By 1980, I had switched from my first horn, the clarinet, to the saxophone (alto, then tenor), and I paid most attention to the horn players. Some nights I heard Willis "Gator Tail" Jackson bar-honk his way through the blues; other times I'd hear former Ellington and Basie band members, players like multi-reedman Russell Procope and tenor saxophonist Harold Ashby. And with some frequency, a hungry Big Joe Turner arrived for a late set, ate a pizza, and then thundered choruses of "Roll 'em, Pete," "Flip, Flop, and Fly," or "Cherry Red":

    Now you can take me

                pretty mama,

>     roll me in yo' big brass bed.
>     I want you to
> >         boogie my woogie,
>     Till my cheeks turn
> >             cherry rehhhhhhhd,
>     cherry red.

When he'd leave the stand, I'd yell and yell—everybody yelled—and sometimes we got another song or two.

Most frequently, I heard the tenor player Percy France and the bebop pianist Joe Albany, who looked as though he'd been punched in the face every night of his life. I don't remember seeing photographers, but 1980 was also the year of Albany's "comeback" documentary, *Joe Albany . . . A Jazz Life*, in which he talks about his hopeless years—how his second wife kills herself, how the third tries to OD, how his own drug use left him in a swamp of irresponsibility (he recorded only once between 1946 and 1971). I don't know whether Albany noticed me, but some nights I'd be half his audience, and once I asked if I could join him at his table between sets, and he said that was cool. The waitress brought him fish and chips.

"I like fish," he said to me. "For a long time, I couldn't get a good fish. It's not so bad here." Not deep fried, no ginger or soy sauce—just wet cubes of pasty flesh. At that moment, nothing in the world seemed sadder.

One evening in 1981, I found enough courage to bring my tenor saxophone and ask Percy France, a sideman that night for Sammy Price, if I could sit in with the band. He checked it out with Price and said he'd give me the nod in the second set. Peck Morrison was on bass, Billy Hart on drums. When France motioned for me to join them, I felt so sick I didn't think I'd be able to blow a single note, but we played a blues, my choice of key, and when we traded fours, France didn't bother to cut me up. He knew that would be too easy. I can't imagine that I played very well, but when we finished, Sammy Price leaned into the microphone and said, "Let's give a hand for Youngblood." Even now, their generosity makes me grin and shake my head.

Sometime later, when I began to consider poetry as a dual center of my life, I described that evening. The poem was 100 percent autobiographical and I thought it captured the anxiety and joy of the event. It didn't. It was an awful poem—and failing in that way made me feel that I'd met my twin in William Matthews's "Mingus at The Showplace":

> I was miserable, of course, for I was seventeen,
> and so I swung into action and wrote a poem,
>
> and it was miserable, for that was how I thought
> poetry worked: you digested experience and shat
>
> literature.

A few lines later, the speaker shows Charles Mingus the poem, and the great jazz bassist responds, "There's a lot of that going around." The poem concludes:

> He glowered
> at me but he didn't look as if he thought
>
> bad poems were dangerous, the way some poets do.
> If they were baseball executives they'd plot
>
> to destroy sandlots everywhere so that the game
> could be saved from children. Of course later
>
> that night he fired his pianist in mid-number
> and flurried him from the stand.
>
> "We've suffered a diminuendo in personnel,"
> he explained, and the band played on.

Mingus could have been blistering to young Bill, and the poem has a built-in sense of gratitude. And similarly, what I learned most from sitting in with Percy France and Sammy Price was not so much the act itself—that I could and did play—but that they accepted what I was able to do at that time. At the West End, the famous people were not so famous (even if they seemed mythic to me), and anyone who wanted to remain anonymous could slouch within a booth or drink at the deep end of the bar. Who knows what I wanted to be, or even become, but I went regularly to hear the music. Nobody knew me, but it was enough—much more than enough—to feel the need to be there.

☙

When my seventeenth birthday approached, my father asked what I wanted and, for a change, I had a suggestion: enough cash to host three friends at the West End. (My father welcomed this idea; he spent all of his "free" time attending to my mother's terminal illness.) My friends were new and a year older—high school seniors who, I later found out, had been instructed by an English teacher to include me in gatherings because I was a loner and my situation was known. On the night of March 14, they arrived as a group, and I enjoyed introducing them to my father.

Josh was a tall fellow with tight curls and a smile that always seemed to say, "I'm a good guy. You can trust me." I knew he had personal battles with his father—a man in politics who began as a philanthropist and then succumbed to the Reagan regime—but Josh rarely let on that this made him ache. Karen played a pretty good piano, and sometimes we'd get together for "Tin Roof Blues" or the adagio from Mozart's clarinet concerto. When she braided her hair, she looked like a Native American princess. Equally beautiful but in a blonde, Nordic way, Brita played flute as well as piano and saxophone; one had the sense she could play anything she wanted. I found her wildly attractive.

Just before we left the house, my mother called from her bedroom, and when I turned, I saw her standing—leaning against the doorjamb but standing on her own, with my grandmother two steps behind, poised to catch her if she lost her balance. She wore a colorful dress (how long had that taken?), and my grandmother had combed her hair for her. The light in the doorway, no doubt dimmed by my mother's instruction, left her in near shadow so that the dress and the shimmers of hair drew our eyes away from her skeletal face and frame. I know she wished us well. I think she even raised a hand to wave.

("Sleep well," I used to tell her every night, even though both of us knew better. *Sleep well.* Those must have been my last words.)

Although that evening I didn't allow myself to meditate on my mother's state of mind, I realize now how fully conscious she must have been of her imminent death, how she knew, for example, that she would not be alive for my next birthday. I suspect that, when we left, she agonized over forthcoming milestones: graduations, marriage, grandchildren. But she shared none of her sorrow—that night or any other. Only once did she begin such a conversation. "Oh, Sascha," she said, late into her illness. "There's so much I want to tell you." But then she became teary, and I said, "I know."

On the walk to the West End, Karen tried to be encouraging about the cancer, how great it was that my mother could get out of bed, but I couldn't talk about it. I didn't allow myself to think of her pain, or even her courage. Worse, I felt angered by the display, as if my new friends would think, "Hey, it's not so bad at his house," and abandon me. I kept thinking, "I don't want to dwell on this tonight. If only for one evening, I want it all to disappear." Then someone started talking about being seventeen, and someone hugged me, and someone else asked a jazz question, and pretty soon we arrived at the club.

Before that evening, I almost always went to the West End alone, and most often I didn't drink booze, though I could. (The drinking age was eighteen, but in New York nobody seemed to care if you were shy a couple of years and kept to yourself.) I ushered Josh, Karen, and Brita past the eatery and into the back room, which featured, at opposite ends, a bar and a small stage. Tables filled the center but we took a booth against the wall, not far from the pianist's left hand. I think my waitress never imagined that I could *have* friends, so when I ordered beers for the table, she gave me a wide smile. I felt I owned the joint.

At that time, I knew nothing about Phil Schaap, the club's emcee. He had not yet won Grammy awards for his liner notes, and he wasn't known as a historian, either, since this predated CDs and his work in record studio vaults, research that would later enrich my understanding of jazz. Should I admit that I thought he was merely thin and boring? It seemed as though whole concerts could be performed within the pauses of his clichéd delivery: "Ladies and . . . gentlemen," "proud . . . to present," "one-n-only." Josh said something like, "Sascha, get up on that stage and teach this guy how to talk," and I grinned, trying to be the cool one. Didn't I know that Schaap was centrally responsible for hiring, and in some cases rediscovering, these musicians? Wasn't I smart enough to assume a reason for his role as announcer? No. I knew nothing about running a club—any club, much less a NYC jazz club in the "Jazz Is Dead" '70s.

The band that night featured Howard McGhee, a terrific trumpeter who had recorded with Charlie Parker in the mid-1940s for labels such as Dial, Stash, and Verve. Wearing shades beneath the brown lights of the club, he still had the look of a '50s hipster, and my eyes kept following the map of his face, badly pockmarked and grooved by years of heroin. He was the headliner, and a virtual unknown outside of jazz circles.

Joe Albany played piano that night, but the other names escaped me, which is why, twenty years later, I telephoned Phil Schaap to see if he could conjure the lineup. Immediately he recalled the tribute, but not even Schaap could remember the bass player (Jeff Fuller, I later discovered) or drummer (Shelton Gary). The alto player, he thought, could possibly have been Dickey Myers, an obscure saxophonist who gigged around town in those days. Much later, Jeff Fuller confirmed Myers had indeed been in the front line with McGhee.

Myers, in fact, got most of my attention. Was he better than McGhee? No, and probably not as good. But I played the saxophone, too, and here was someone who could invoke Charlie Parker—who knew the tunes, knew the bop cadences—and he seemed so damn *happy* to be there. If Josh or Brita or Karen spoke during the first set, I did not hear them. I'm not sure if I've ever been more lost in music.

And where did Howard McGhee's memory travel through the chasmic silences of Schaap's break notices? What fragments from the announcer's microphone lingered? "Bird," "Bird Lives," "McGhee, who recorded," "Legend," "Dial Sessions," "tonight, so proud," "back soon." Maybe, at least for a moment, McGhee fell back to July 29, 1946, when a twenty-five-year-old Parker drank a quart of whisky in a failed effort to settle himself for a studio recording. Joe Albany had been slotted to play piano for that infamous gig at Dial (he fought with Bird the night before and quit the band), but McGhee was there and had helped arrange the recording. They cut only four tunes: "Max Making Wax," "Lover Man," "The Gypsy," and "Bebop." How Parker was able to play at all is something of a medical miracle, no matter what version of the story you believe. Some say he took fistfuls of Benzedrine all week and was suffering from withdrawal; some say he couldn't score enough heroin and was jonesing from the little he had in his system. Some say he got six phenobarbital tablets at the gig itself. McGhee's version is more to the point: "He was in trouble. . . . His horn was shooting up in the air and he couldn't stand still, he couldn't sit down. . . . He didn't know what to do."

It was McGhee who tried to salvage the session, and McGhee who got the call that, after Parker left the studio, he'd gotten into trouble at the Civic Hotel. Fire. Bird had burned the room, or was it a cigarette smoldering on the mattress, or was there really a fire at all? (McGhee said he never saw any signs.) And Bird was naked, though where they found him also changes from account to account—in his bedroom, in the hotel lobby, in his car, on top of his car. (What version of the story should we believe?) McGhee drives to the hotel, but Parker's already in police custody, sent to Camarillo State Hospital, where he'll stay for six months. According to McGhee, Bird had already calmed down by the time he found him:

> *McGhee:* Damn, what's goin' on, man?
>
> *Parker:* Oh, everything's fine, everything's fine. Give me my clothes. I want to get out of here.
>
> *McGhee:* Well, it ain't quite like that, Bird. I can't get you out like that. You have to go to court and all that shit. I don't know what the fuck they got against you, but they got something against you. It sounds kind of bad.

As for the recordings from that afternoon, Parker later called them "my worst on wax. . . . They were all awful." And how could they be otherwise? He was spinning—spinning away from the booth, his horn oscillating the way the room should have spun for someone who'd finished a quart of whisky. Then, and forever on record, he misses the entrance to "Lover Man," and when he reaches for his first major run, his horn—did he arc it to the side or turn his back to the microphone?—drops out of tune. Doppler effect.

I didn't know any of this that night at the West End when they featured Dickey Myers on "Lover Man," nor can I offer a telling detail about McGhee's reaction; he simply announced the ballad feature and left the stand for a round at the bar. Had the thirty-four years dulled the ache of those Dial sessions, or would a rendition like this, with cascading Bird-influenced lines, jigsaw McGhee's memory? Doppler effect: *everything's fine, everything's fine.* Tune coming to a close. *You have to go to court and all that shit.* Shelton Gary motioning to the bar. *Damn, what's goin' on, man?* Someone yells, "Bird Lives!" *It sounds kind of bad.* "Welcome back to the stage, a living legend . . ." *Well, it ain't quite like that, Bird.* Sotto voce: "Let's end the set with something fast. Anything fast." *Give me my clothes. I want to get out of here.*

"52nd Street Theme." Break.

My friends came back into focus. We had another round of cold beer, and they wished me happy birthday again.

"You should ask the sax player if you can study with him," Brita said, and Karen thought that was an outstanding idea.

"Yes, definitely," she said.

I saw the band members grouped near the bar and walked over. I said they were wonderful and asked Myers whether he gave lessons.

"Yeah," he said, mildly interested. "You can call me if you want," but then he leapt from the topic and threw his arm around McGhee. Suddenly he got all sugared up.

"This is the *man*," he said, beaming now. "It's such an honor to be here with him. I'm so humbled." McGhee smiled, looked down, looked away, said nothing. "I mean, this guy *played* with Bird, you know? This guy's my *hero*."

It was my cue to say something nice about Howard McGhee. But I didn't quite know how to respond. I mentioned that my father had loaned me the Savoy sessions that featured him with Parker, but, unintentionally, I'd created a bizarre time shift: 1946, 1980. McGhee looked at me—thin and white, eager but near mute—and lost interest immediately. What could I possibly know about jazz or a jazz life? Hell, where was Howard McGhee in the consciousness of America?

At this point, memory jump-cuts like a scratch on a record; I can't recall saying goodbye or walking away. But when I returned to the table, Josh seemed very excited. He didn't think I'd actually approach them, and he wanted to know all about the encounter—not because he cared about jazz musicians, but because he cared about me. (I know that now.) Karen and Brita encouraged me to pursue the private lessons, and I told them I'd think about it. For me, though, it was enough that I had thanked them for playing. It would be the first time among many where I'd be amazed that the audience hadn't mobbed the band and that no one, in fact, paid them any attention whatsoever.

In the late 1980s, the West End Jazz Café changed its name to the West Gate and moved a block north before folding. Most of the players I used to hear are gone, too. Howard McGhee died in 1987, aged sixty-nine. As of today, only four of his records remain in print, the last from 1976. Joe Albany died in 1988, shortly before his sixty-fourth birthday; he has about four CDs as well. As for saxophonist Dickey Myers, I know only this: no recordings are available (not even with him as a sideman), and he died in 1992, unknown even to most jazz aficionados. That same year, Percy France died after being hit by a car in New York City; again, only a couple recordings exist on CD.

My three friends attended different colleges while I finished my final year of high school. I'm not sure whether Josh fully resolved his differences with his father but, with rather astonishing circularity, we ended up a quarter of a century later in neighboring summer homes. He'd lost touch with Karen and Brita, too. Someone told me Karen moved to Indonesia and founded a school in Bali. As for Brita, I heard she married well and now spends half the year Europe, though I've never followed this up. Some things, I think, should be left in the time where they grew, and I'm comfortable leaving them there in the West End's wooden booth.

That night, I learned the importance of hearing music with others, even if nobody says anything. I witnessed the essence of courage: my mother walking on her own for the last time, laboring to give everyone a sense of hope for a full evening. I experienced the pleasure of being a host, even if I only had a two-beer tolerance. But most of all, I remember the quintet itself, the front line of saxophone and trumpet, those bebop tunes and phrases I didn't even know I knew by heart. Throughout the evening, my collapsing life at home transformed into a world of sound as the spirit of Charlie Parker flooded the horns. McGhee no longer had to mourn a loved friend; Bird was *there*, and we were there to hear the room become the tunes themselves: "Hot House," "Cool Blues," "Confirmation," "Parker's Mood," "Now's the Time," "Dizzy Atmosphere," "All the Things You Are," "Groovin' High." To imagine my fingers on the keys, my lips around the mouthpiece of a saxophone, all I had to do was close my eyes.

I'm closing them now.

# Spells

The obituary in the *New York Times* ran on April 17, 1980, two days after my mother died. My father bought many copies of the paper, and although I'm sure I read it, that experience has left me. I do remember having no interest in the piece, and only recently did I bother to scan through the spools of microfilm at our library and reread the obit:

> Anita Askild Feinstein, a painter, designer and weaver, died of cancer at her home in Manhattan Tuesday. She was 47 years old.
>
> Until last June, Miss Askild had taught textile design at Pratt Institute. Her own design for Jack Lenor Larsen, "Caravan," has become a classic in his textile collections.
>
> Miss Askild's paintings, which are in a number of private and public collections, have won awards in New York, Philadelphia, Cape Cod and Sweden. Her weavings were shown at the Museum of Contemporary Crafts in New York and have been featured in *Time* and *Life* magazines and in *Woman's Wear Daily*.

> Born in Sweden, Miss Askild trained at the Konstfack, the Stockholm arts academy. Coming to this country in her mid-20s, she studied painting with the late Hans Hofmann and with Sam Feinstein, to whom she was married in 1963.
>
> Besides her husband, Miss Askild is survived by a son, Sascha Feinstein; her mother and two brothers.

Most of this brief profile offers accurate details. She did arrive in America while in her twenties, though she first visited on her own when she was seventeen (a bold journey for the only young woman in her family; even today, with numerous extensions of that family tree, no one else has ventured to live outside of Sweden). Her design titled "Caravan" sustained its popularity in the Larsen line for decades, though she worked many more years for Gloria Bucé Associates, and I think she would have wanted Gloria to be acknowledged. I'm sorry, too, that the *Times* listed the marriage year as 1963 and not 1962; taken as fact, it suggests I was a child born out of wedlock.

But the most unsettling quality to this obituary, and most others, is its lack of spirit. In briefly summing up notices and awards, the text does exactly what it's not supposed to do: it makes a person inorganic. It dismisses soul. It takes all the best parts of our humanity—humor and generosity and forgiveness, not to mention the vitality that drives a creative spirit—and levels it flush to the page. It acts, as my friend Jon once pointed out, as a useless résumé.

On the surface, obituaries tell readers why they should care about the deceased, but the stagnancy of time markers freezes the wonderful elasticity of time itself. Shouldn't language do more than that, and isn't that one way to judge writing? A strong artist's best work takes the past and reinvents it with renewed vigor, so that it becomes simultaneously a commentary on what came before, what's happening at the moment, and what can or will take place in the future. Necessarily bland and objective, the words of my mother's obituary belong in their antiseptic home: at the center of a thick roll of plastic film, stuffed in a carton that looks exactly like hundreds of others, and filed within a large beige cabinet.

What I do like about the notice is that it touches on my mother's breadth as an artist, her range of talents: the paintings and weavings and textile designs. But the list could have been much longer. She made excellent photographs, developing and printing her work, and was frequently encouraged to send out her images for publication, though that didn't interest her in the slightest. She made clothes, including a series of dresses with woven panels down the front. (Again, friends encouraged her to produce them in a commercial line, but she didn't have the time for mass production.) She worked well with clay, creating realistic busts and abstract plaques, as well as more standard forms. Because of her skillful hand and artistic eye, our barren courtyard behind the brownstone became a tulip sanctuary, and during summers, when we stayed on Cape Cod, much larger gardens flourished.

During those summers, she often held workshops for children. One year, for example, she taught kids how to make marionettes—the whole process, from painted papier-mâché heads to dowel-stick skeletons and sewn clothes. She made animated films and taught workshops on that as well. Often she'd write scripts for the children in the neighborhood and would film them, the final edits screened at a big party in late August. Until her illness, I don't recall any stretch of time when she wasn't using her hands to make something of this world.

Although not a writer, and not known by anyone for her writing, she wrote three children's books, all self-illustrated and unpublished. The earliest, called *Spells*, has eight pages of sewn felt on cardboard. Each page illustrates a particular noun, with block letters cut from the fabric to suggest puzzle pieces, such as BIRD (side view of a chubby cardinal with magenta wings beside a red tulip), or HORSE (green body, blue mane). The effect: Letters belong here; together, they make words; words let your mind travel. We identify the unusually colored horse as a horse because of its shape; because we know it as HORSE, we accept its green hide. Invisible letters to fill cut guides. Bold words beneath each soft collage. It's a charming book.

The second work's more personalized—almost embarrassingly so—and she titled it *My Name Is Sascha*. It's also made with cut felt on cardboard, and the illustrations, like each year of my childhood, depict New York City (autumn to spring) and Cape Cod (summer). In one illustration, I'm whistling to a moon and stars, "Waking up the day"; in another, I'm peering through waist-deep water, amazed at my foreshortened legs. In my daughter's favorite collage, "I tried some hocus-pocus / Digging up the garden crocus": beneath a purple hat and a coat with orange buttons, I scoop pink tulips from a wide expanse of green and toss them overhead.

I can only vaguely recall being read those two books, but the third I remember vividly. My mother made the book in 1971, when I was eight. She woke up one morning with the entire plot in her head and wrote it in one sitting. Later she rewrote the text as rhymed passages (many of them forced, since Swedish was her first language). To accompany the narrative, she drew pictures with extra fine tipped pens and bold watercolors, charging the words with elegant and vibrant illustrations. It was the story of a boy fated by nature (a storm) and supernatural forces (the mythical Scandinavian Norns) to be isolated; then he encounters an astonishing woman who unravels and reverses his fate. My mother named this boy Anders—my middle name—and titled the story *Anders and the Norns*.

A family friend, tangentially involved in the book business, tried to get it published, but this never happened. One commercial house said the story would be too scary for kids; another thought the color illustrations would be too expensive to reproduce. And though some people asked about the project from time to time, nothing more happened. Nor was this by any means the focus of my mother's creative life; the lack of professional recognition for *Anders and the Norns* meant very little to her. Once she became ill, we forgot entirely about the book. But before I went to college, I asked my father where it had been stored, and this request became the start of a strange and wonderful journey.

My father knew the book had been stored "in a very safe place," a line I'd learned to distrust since childhood. In the four-story brownstone where I was raised, anything could get lost, and we rarely found things quickly. The building included a large basement where he taught his art classes—in essence, a fifth floor—and on the fourth floor he painted. In that top floor studio, my father kept many, many things besides paintings, and all of them were important to him, though no one would guess by looking. He thought the book would be in his studio, so when I came to visit at Thanksgiving of my college freshman year, we walked the four flights and began our search.

How can I begin to describe the search itself? For decades—long before I was born—my father collected shards from New York City, and every city through which he traveled, so that this room, and most in the house, had become a living sculpture. Visitors to his studio—on the rare occasions when he allowed visitors—always failed to visualize how he painted in an area reduced exponentially in size. In a very literal sense, the walls in that house moved towards the center by inches and feet. Almost everyone who first encounters my father's house says, "I've never seen anything like this."

Let me offer an example of the pack-rat structure. Two reasonably sized rooms on that fourth floor—one on each end of the landing—have been fully loaded: bottom to top, front to back. No one can see the doors to these rooms, however, because, on the outside, stacked boxes rise from floor to ceiling. I do not know what exactly has been preserved in those rooms; I've only once witnessed the contents, and from a distance. And I didn't even know the rooms *existed* until I was fifteen.

Once I walked down to the cellar at the moment when my father emerged from within a still life. (The still life itself wraps the cellar's perimeter and grows out from the walls; the displays change several times annually, objects adjusted in the name of inspiration but also in the need of storage.) He had been in yet another room obscured from everyone's view; even today, like overgrown ruins in Mexico, the entrance to this room does not appear to exist. But the room itself must have some substantive dimension, because at one point it housed forty or fifty old wooden sewing machine boards—each a different size and approximately two inches thick. (In the modern age of plastic, sewing factories began to toss out the original wooden bases, and my father collected all he could, moving hundreds of pounds of wood from one loft to the next, and again to the basement of his brownstone.) A dozen years later, he unearthed these blocks, sanded them down, bolted them into the kitchen floor, filled the bolt holes and cracks with a mixture of saw dust and polyurethane, and then urethaned the floor itself. The unqualified success of such projects allowed him to justify every ounce of clutter.

This also meant, however, that no place was "a safe place."

Our search for *Anders and the Norns* began in his studio, where he recalled a particular cabinet. "I would have put it there," he said. To reach the cabinet, we labored through various barriers (doors, planks, dismantled boxes, metal sheets) before reaching the smaller, more portable objects: wooden handles from snapped hammers; cracked plastic inserts from air conditioners we never owned; the steering section of a Volkswagen; art supply receipts from the 1950s; stalagmites of books on painting, music, archery, radio signals, acupuncture, taxes, lost civilizations, found civilizations, and so on; bits of a Greek sculpture and one plaster cast of David's head; piping and siding; a small bag filled with what was probably cement (and that surprised us with a bloom of dust); bent nails, cracked ratchets, stripped screws, busted hasps.

We did not find the book. When we got to the cabinet, we discovered that of the six thin drawers, two did not exist, one was empty (empty!), one had a collection of string and rubber bands, and the last two had things I could never imagine keeping. In disbelief, I lifted out some of the objects. My father looked confused and distracted. "I know it's around here," he kept saying. "I know I protected it." I didn't say anything and slowly began to replace the unearthed materials. But when I picked up a small block of wood—two inches by three—I felt the cool, smooth surprise of metal, and turned it over.

The image in the copper had been etched in the early thirties. It approximated the look of a daguerreotype but without the immediate luminosity. I later learned the proper term—*photogravure*—and the process of transferring a photograph to a copper plate, which is finely etched so that ink can blacken the darkest parts of the portrait. Invented in 1879, the process became highly refined but lost favor mainly because of the expensive transfer.

The etched metal therefore created a photographic negative, and yet I could still recognize the faint image. I handed the printing block to my father.

"Oh yeah," he said. "This was my high school portrait."

I held it in my palm the way one might hold a fallen bird. My father could almost remember the full story behind the image, but he was curiously dismissive; he was glad to have it, glad I found it, but, for him, it seemed to have a value equal to everything else we uncovered. Maybe that's why he so readily let me keep the portrait, which now sits on a shelf above my writing desk, and for the rest of that afternoon, I kept turning the image in my hands. At an angle, from above and in near shadow, the portrait became fully photographic. Tipped into sunlight: a copper ghost.

Not finding the book disappointed me and pained my father; he knew he had handled it last, and for a couple of years he would often mention his continued search, insisting that it would be found. "It's probably right under my nose." But it remained sealed within the house, and years disappeared. I graduated from college. My father remarried. I began to find a voice as a writer and went to graduate school to pursue literature and the art of poetry. And it was during orientation—that first session designed to feign welcome and instill terror—where I first saw my wife.

The incoming grad students had been packed into a large amphitheater and sat like statues while the head of graduate studies, a middle-aged man with broken capillaries and bad teeth, droned on about the miserable journey we had chosen: the dismaying job market and devastating forecasts. In essence, he described terminal degrees as being merely terminal, and his gloom began to settle in my frontal lobe. Then, all the way on the other side, across rows and rows of depressed minions, I watched an Indian woman quietly step into the room and slip into a vacant seat. I don't know how many people saw her, but for the next hour, while various professors bludgeoned the audience with grim news, I simply stared at this gorgeous woman, utterly mesmerized and, I like to believe, already in love.

The messengers of doom finally dismissed the group and directed us to a room on the fourth floor where we had to fill out various forms. That's when I charged like a scrawny running back in an effort to "naturally" meet this woman. Standing side by side in a line that wrapped through the hallway, I tried to be extra cool as I introduced myself and asked for her name.

"Marleni," she said, accenting the first syllable and, in a lovely British lilt, converting the *r* to an *h*.

"Beautiful," I replied, though I was already at a loss, having not quite registered the name. "Where are you from?"

"Singapore."

"Ah, Singapore," I said. (I wanted to sound internationally hip, though I knew nothing about the country and immediately flipped through the atlas when I returned to my apartment.) After that first encounter, our courses interlocked starting with a Shakespeare seminar, and we began to date. In my favorite photograph of her from that first year, she's in the center of seasonal change—an entirely new experience for her: Indian starlet cross-legged on the lawn, hair shimmering around her face towards the spectacle of autumn.

Marleni made me reconsider the seasons, and by winter I could not imagine my life without her. I visited her family that June, in Singapore, and though they checked me out *thoroughly* ("What did you expect?" she'd say to me, laughing), they never criticized the romance because of race. During that visit, I also traveled to Malaysia and Thailand and Indonesia, and these new landscapes and cultures began to reshape my whole world—love and family, art and nature, ceremony and spirit.

I also began to reconsider previous experiences and tried to write, for example, about the photogravure—receiving the unexpected gift, the possible necessity of sacrificing one treasured object for another—but the ideas seemed forced and the poem did not work very well. Recalling the search for *Anders and the Norns*, however, brought me back to the story itself. I tried to reclaim the book's history through the memory of each colored page, and as I began to reconsider the narrative, I realized for the first time an astonishing parallel with my own life. The lines came quickly, and then I pushed them into soft rhymes to approximate the fairy-tale tone:

## Anders and the Norns
### — *for Anita*

The fairy tale wrote itself from a dream,
you said, and your illustrations bloomed
to the cover: my middle name,
Anders, in tall letters circled with blue.

Above the mountains, three Norns
whispered as they spun the lifelines
that guide our journey. One night, a storm
swept the peaks, whirlwinded their twine

into hard knots: a child born backward
in manners, stuttering, though he sang
his youth with the forest's birds—
tanagers, parakeets, toucans.

Coming home one day, he saw black wings
and a huge beak pulling the line's end,
took hold of the last knot, and, flying
now, soared over houses, an ocean.

They glided to an island called *Wish*
where he met a king and his daughter
who had chestnut-colored skin. The princess
untangled the line until his stutter

disappeared, and they fell in love. Anders
made a wedding dress for her sewn
from the island's large white flowers,
and she wove a suit from his own yarn.

After you died, we packed the book away
but I've wondered as the years passed
how you could have known that day
what I couldn't have known to ask:

> Did you see my future appear
>
> in the vision before your death?
>
> For I'm in love with a woman whose hair
>
> drifts down her back like tapestry threads,
>
> her skin dark brown, her home an island
>
> halfway around the world. In dreams
>
> she's curled her fingers into your hand,
>
> the two of you rising over vast green seas.

The suggestion of foreseeable futures allowed the poem to become a poem, to reach beyond a mere retelling of memory. I began to think more consciously about vision and spiritual connections, about important, impossible questions. It was enough, I thought, to raise the possibility of psychic vision; I saw no need to mention the fact that by packing the book away we had lost it.

*Spells* and *My Name Is Sascha* came back into my life too late to read to my son, but I used to read them to my daughter, who asked for them frequently. Although she knew my mother created the stories, I assumed my daughter was too young to understand the full sentimental impact of this legacy—and yet, even at the age of three, she made a deep connection:

"Will you read your mother's books?" she asked. "I love those books."

"I'm so pleased to hear that. What do you love about them?"

She looked me in the eyes and said, "They bring me to you."

I was astonished. "What do you mean?"

She couldn't understand what wasn't clear and repeated her phrase, with emphasis: "They bring *me*—to *you*."

When my daughter gets older, I will tell her how we discovered *Spells* behind an expanded wall in a large room of the brownstone that had been my mother's studio. On the second floor, in an effort to compartmentalize more of whatever needed to be kept, my father had hung enormous wooden doors in front of floor-to-ceiling cabinets and shelving. (This took place during my mother's lifetime; I remember her complaining how the doors had not been properly hinged, that they were almost impossible to open, and that she rarely used the space.) But that's where the book remained—in a drawer of a cabinet much like the one in my father's studio where I found the photogravure. Beneath *Spells*, we found an eleven-by-fourteen Aquabee sketch pad with a pen-and-ink cover by Henry Pitz, one of my father's teachers. We had many such pads, and it could easily have been blank or filled with abandoned starts, but it was, in fact, the illustrated text of *Anders and the Norns*.

That book's in my house, too. (My father said he never again wanted such responsibility.) With the original work in hand, I'm pleased to know that my poem reflects the book's imagery fairly accurately, and what's wrong isn't terribly wrong. But I know why poets often wish they were painters. How can words capture colors? The Norns sit beneath a phosphorous orange sky. The head of the bird that first brings Anders to his disappointed family bristles with hundreds of fine pen strokes. When Anders learns of his stolen yarn, he rides home on a giant deer by clutching a rack of gnarled brown horns, and later in the story, when he awakes to the princess, she's wearing a dress that's as blue as a simple truth.

The glue used to paste in the text has dried, and some of the words float loosely within the pages, and some of the pages themselves have separated from the spine. But I will find a way to preserve this story so that my daughter, whose middle name is Anita, and my son, whose middle name is Anders, can read the book to their children. They'll see a boy changed forever when a princess, using a strength she never knew she embodied, pulls Anders through the arched window of her turret, just hours before unraveling his tangled lifeline and leading him into a new, multicolored world.

# The Pheasant's Reflection 🔥

How was it possible, even in my dimmest of memories, to confuse the two subway stations—one at 168th, beneath Columbia Presbyterian Hospital, and the other at 190th and Fort Tryon Park, the exit for the Cloisters? The first I visited several times in 1977, when my father had a heart attack, and again in 1979, when my mother first learned of her cancer. I knew the second station less well; my mother often took me to the Cloisters when I was a child, but we usually traveled by bus, not train. Perhaps this seems inconsequential—the confusion, I mean—but these stations evoked such emotional extremes: from one location, I entered a massive, dark, towering hospital; from the other, I walked joyfully to an expansive, serene, castlelike monastery. I hated that I could not distinguish between the two.

But I now understand why. In both stations, passengers must exit in an elevator, which is unusual for the New York transit system. I could recall quite clearly the slow-motion speed of a subway elevator, even the smell of oil and old steel, but I had repressed the travels to Columbia Presbyterian, and so my mind fused the nightmarish imagery: one hundred or more feet below the earth, I walk from the train to charcoal-colored elevators—the relics of a world war, it seemed—and then, very slowly, as I pray to some anonymous god that a mugger not slip between the closing doors, the elevator jerks and rises to ground level.

Revisiting the hospital station at 168th, I found myself strangely removed from associative responses, at least initially. Compared to so many other stations, this locale retains a historical dignity, though some of the history's been altered for the sake of safety: they've modernized and relocated the elevators. But they've retained the essence of New York's duality, in this case a setting that's half romance novel, half murder mystery. If you pause on one of the bridges above the trains—an unusual feature that allows people to cross from one side of the tracks to the other—you can still observe dirt-encrusted florets embedded in the ceiling.

Those details never emerged when I was sixteen, en route to the hospital, my eyes glazed and unaware. What did I remember? The glow: the walls of ghostly white globes filled with mercury vapor, globes glowing along the walls, globes glowing along the bridge. I stared at the tops of two trains, both pulling away from the station, one heading north, the other south, and then I stared at the lights, collectively, then individually. Soot and dirt had coagulated with humidity and heat, and black rivulets streaked each lamp. For a few minutes, my eyes couldn't take in anything else.

From 168th, I switched to the A train and got off at 190th, one of the deepest tunnels in the city (about 140 feet down) and one that twists through rock, its path far more snakelike than the lines in downtown Manhattan. Some passengers took the winding exit that rises to street level, but the rest of us waited for the elevators, also renovated, that ascend through rock. Above, various paths crisscross through Fort Tryon Park and lead circuitously to the Cloisters. The Hudson flows to the left. Across the river: relatively unspoiled Jersey landscape. The whole experience approximates Persephone's mythic journey from the world of Hades into springtime.

I now find it difficult to disassociate that ascent to the Cloisters from the museum itself, which houses the magnificent Unicorn Tapestries. As a kid, I loved the narratives that these tapestries inspired, but I felt disconnected from the artists' religious intentions—historical context, or art as artifact. Perhaps that's one reason why I so admire William Olsen's poem titled "The Unicorn Tapestries":

> The things we leave behind must, for those
> who find them flattened, scentless inside books
> or in a gesture they make that isn't theirs,
> be very much like the desk I found in the alley
> one night, coming out of one way down another,
>
> when I couldn't sleep or write letters, and walked.
> The desk had lost a leg, and couldn't get away.
> Some initials cut through oak had outlasted love.
> Turning over the drawer to interpret
> the contents, I thought of the farmer centuries ago
> and the stack of "curtains" he found in a chest.
> All the crazy things he couldn't understand—
>
> the unicorn, Christ reborn; the seductive
> damsel, Mary, who lured Him into the circular fence,
> Her dress lifted ever so slightly, Her glance askew,
> His smiling as if all the world centered on Him,
> a field of lilies, violets, passionate roses
> and periwinkles, "joy of the ground"—
>
> he took them to the barn to cover the potatoes.
> Little worked that winter. The potatoes darkened
> the light that hid inside them. They grew eyes
> until they were nothing but vision drained of life:
> the unicorn bleeding and braying all winter
> as the farmer lifted it and saw his work
>
> ruined, for all his efforts.

Unlike the farmer, I had many imaginative avenues into these woven narratives, and, even as a child, I recoiled at the thought of the tapestries being abandoned and nearly destroyed by neglect. I also loved the monastery just as much as the art work, particularly the chamber with a vaulted ceiling, its lines curved and curving within curves the way medieval scribes patterned the margins of illuminated manuscripts. Standing beneath stone archways, or outside overlooking the Hudson, I could easily fall into the role of prince or knight.

I suppose one might say I role-played a knight once again when I traveled to Columbia Presbyterian Hospital in 1979, so caught up in bravery that I would later suppress all memory of those visits. Nor do I remember when my father first discussed the diagnosis with my mother, and I never asked about that conversation. Initially, I didn't want to know her response; later, I didn't want him to relive the moment. Recalling those weeks, however, I find it startling to remember how the first diagnosis was *not* unbearably grim; they'd discovered cancer in a lymph node on her neck and, I was told, assumed that cancerous cells had collected only in that tiny area—because other tests kept returning negative. No signs in the liver. No signs in the kidneys. Stomach, spleen—who knows what else. By mid-October, when the doctors finally determined my mother had ovarian cancer, the disease had surrounded most of her major organs. Inoperable. But for two or three weeks, I had no reason not to believe that radiation treatments could annihilate whatever minute amounts remained once the lymph node was removed.

I remember quite vividly sitting in the high school cafeteria with my teacher for a class called "British Authors," how he asked politely about my parents—just to get to know me better—and how I nervously unfurled the details of my mother's condition, emphasizing the fact that the hospital had found "microscopic traces." I always quoted that phrase, steadying myself on the syllables of "microscopic" so that I could believe the word. And I remember being puzzled by his response, because he looked so serious and said things such as, "Oh, I'm so sorry." Hadn't he heard me? I repeated myself ("They're certain radiation will cure this . . ."), and though he didn't respond verbally, I chose to interpret his expression as a smile.

For the final six months of her life, my mother remained in our home, but in September and October she made several trips to Columbia Presbyterian, and for at least two stretches she remained overnight, including the evening of October 2, her forty-seventh birthday. The staff permitted my father and me to stay beyond the usual visiting period, and my memories of that night emerge from subway-like color and lighting: the corridors blackened except for emergency exit signs and, inside the room, a strip of fluorescent light over my mother's bed, our outlines awash in a yellow never meant for the living or the dying.

We'd brought presents—mainly art books—and my gift was *The Visconti Hours*, a book of hours illuminated at the turn of the fifteenth century, roughly a hundred years before the making of the Unicorn Tapestries. Days before, I'd gone downtown to buy *Les Très Riches Heures du Duc de Berry*, which I had seen and admired, but when I leafed through various illuminated manuscripts, the collection commissioned by the Visconti literally outshined all others. Chestnut castles within jade forests. Lapis calligraphy. Scarlet climbing ivy. Lambs and lightning, Gods and sinners, golden halos and golden profiles and shimmering golden auras. Every page—even the depiction of the "Fall of the Rebel Angels," where four celestial beings spear a golden devil, and where brown, dragon-shaped creatures fall in flames from the sky—appeared to be a blessing.

Known to be overly generous in her praise and thanks, my mother must have thanked me effusively, but I have no memory of our conversation. Not a sentence. I remember the good feeling I had in giving this particular book, but most of all, my mind's telephoto lens rephotographs the one-inch scar on her neck, where they extracted the node for a biopsy. I had told myself not to look—or at least not to get caught looking—but every time I thought my mother wasn't watching, my eyes studied the incision.

Was this the evening my throat dried? The hallway: I'm walking towards vending machines that glow with shocking vibrancy—bright whites and blues, bright red across my hands as I sift through coins. My back tightens like a muscle spasm when the Coke thumps to the base of the dispenser. I turn around, and my vision's still streaked. Then: the chiaroscuro of a white gown heading to my mother's room, and I stop the doctor, almost forcefully.

"I'm Anita Feinstein's son."

"Good to meet you," he says.

"The cancer—in the lymph node—" My mind again reforms the scar, the doctor's presence fully eclipsed by that minor incision. "That's from microscopic sources, right?"

"As far as we know, yes."

"And that can be treated, right? It's microscopic."

"That's what we think."

He hadn't lied to me, but his answers sealed a disbelief in danger, the early stage of a profound closure, and I kept replaying his words as he visited my parents. I stood in the hall, gulping at first from the can, then sipping more slowly so that the sugared bubbles fizzed on my tongue. My parents would probably ask for the same kind of confirmation, and maybe my mother would feel assured of a healthy prognosis and weep, and I didn't want to be there for that. And I'd be lying if I didn't admit to feeling relief when the staff changed shifts and a nurse said to my father, "You'll have to leave now. It's after hours."

Twenty years later, I'm back in New York City, sifting through a cabinet filled with my mother's personal belongings, much of which she made. Some drawers contain textiles; others hold the carved woodblocks and linoleum tiles used to create many of the textile designs. One drawer's been stuffed with letters, the majority of them in Swedish—primarily from her mother—and therefore mysterious to me. I find pads filled with a dazzling range of ink drawings, some composed like threads held against a Midwestern sky, others like the densest forest imagery, with creatures and human figures entangled within a fury of trees and shrubbery. I select nine of the best and have them professionally framed. The rest I carefully box and label.

My mother had also selected and gathered a number of photographs, mostly black-and-whites that she had taken—which is another way of saying they're mainly of me, from my first few days to my early teenage years. Only the earliest photographs embarrass me, because I was sensationally ugly at birth; the doctors had pried me out with forceps, causing the left side of my skull to bulge like the Sierra Madres. When my father first saw me, he thought, *Oh, Christ. I'll learn to live with this, but Anita will never recover.* He then went to her room and asked with trepidation, "Have you seen him yet?"

"Yes," my mother replied with a smile. "Isn't he beautiful?"

In the baby photo I know best, my right knee angles into the frame. My father had carried this picture in his wallet. At an art opening not long after my birth, a painter scanned the photo, pointed to my knee, and asked sarcastically, "Is that his penis?" My father replied, "Part of it."

I don't seem to be happy in any of the baby pictures, but I don't seem to be unhappy in any of the others, particularly the ones with my mother. In a portrait that's now framed in my office, it's summertime, I'm about four, and she's holding the kitten we bought that summer, Robin, the only pet I've ever had. I look almost waiflike, my eyes matte black and planetarily dark against my white shirt. But my mother's eyes pull the entire camera lens to her face. She's smiling widely, and it reminds me how I grew into her smile, tooth for tooth.

In all but one photo, she's between the ages of thirty and thirty-six (my first six years), and when people see these portraits, they respond as a virtual collective: "Wow. She was so beautiful." It's difficult, of course, for a son to write about his mother's beauty, but in looking at these various portraits, I'm startled by the *kind* of beauty she embodied: she appears youthful enough to be ten years younger, but her soulful presence generates a sense of wisdom that transcends superficial attractiveness—the kind my generation, and the subsequent ones, popularize.

The vitality of her physical beauty did not necessarily make her death more tragic, but it did cause the reality of her illness to be more incomprehensible for those who knew her. Some literally did not believe that she had died. Some began a quest of profound soul searching, suddenly aware of their own mortality. Some questioned God.

The joy and energy that infused so many of her creative works feel tangible in this handful of captured moments, which is probably why she selected and set aside these particular images of herself. As for the photographs in which we're together, they express far more exactly what I've heard so often, before and after her death: "You two were inseparable." Arranged and rearranged, the snapshots and portraits cascade across my living-room table like stills from a movie. In almost all of them, she's wrapped an arm around me, and I'm staring into the camera with the eyes of a child who couldn't possibly imagine grief.

Among the photographs and letters, I also found five cards, details from unicorn tapestries but without any images of the unicorn itself. The first card presents a passive lioness and an open-mouthed lion, and the second depicts two pheasants at a fountain. These are details from a tapestry at the Cloisters—perhaps my favorite—where men discuss how to begin their hunt. The third postcard portrays an alert dog emerging from bushes, and the fourth focuses on three other hunting dogs, one with an unnaturally long neck held straight like a tower. In the fifth card, a detail from a tapestry in Paris's Musée de Cluny, an elegant woman stands with a parakeet on her gloved hand. In the completed scene, the woman reaches for an enormous chalice held by a servant. A lion and a unicorn, each supporting a staff with a banner depicting the coat of arms, frame the two women, along with small dogs, rabbits, and monkeys. A cheetah reclines in the distance. Birds at rest. Birds in flight.

What details do we select for interpretation? ("The things we leave behind must, for those / who find them flattened, scentless inside books / or in a gesture they make that isn't theirs, / be very much like . . .")

After comparing these images to the whole works, I suspect these cards remained not because my mother cherished them but because they were part of a set and the ones with more dramatic details had been mailed to friends. Where, after all, were the images of the unicorn blending with the white fountain in the second great Cloisters tapestry, or leaping from the river in the third, or goring the hunting dog in the fourth? True, some depictions of the unicorn being slaughtered probably never appeared on postcards. (In the fifth tapestry, its back bleeds from biting hounds; in the sixth, which portrays two scenes, spears pierce the unicorn's breast, and then the body's slung over a horse's back.) But what of the famous seventh tapestry, with the unicorn fenced in yet resurrected, its wounds noticeable but self-healing? Perfect balance, even as a small reproduction. Certainly that would have been part of this set, and didn't its absence mean she gave the unicorn images to others?

What details do we select? ("Turning over the drawer to interpret / the contents, I thought of . . .")

If I'm wrong, and these are not "seconds," perhaps my mother selected these cards because she loved the parts of the world too often neglected. Because she knew the quarter inch of white hair at the bottom of the fourth card is, in fact, part of the unicorn's mane, and that the expressions on at least two of the three dogs, frozen as they witness a horn piercing another's gut, suggest a startled awareness of their own mortality. Because she wanted proof of a weaver's ability to reproduce individual hairs draped from a lion's face or swept across his paws. Because, without detail, we might overlook the fountain's ghosted reflection of the pheasant's green head. Because she knew that in reframing the world, we reframe our selves.

# The Wide Hands of Charles Mingus

"Just promise me this," my father repeated during my adolescence: "Don't take drugs, and don't get married too early." Avoiding drugs seemed clear and unquestionable to me; the second bit of advice just seemed silly, since I didn't know any teenagers who had considered marriage. And didn't my father realize that I was aware of his previous marriages—one in art school that lasted less than a year, and another, much more substantive marriage that preceded the one with my mother? Was he saying his life had been a mistake, or that I should emulate his parental timetable—that is, fathering a child for the first and only time at the age of forty-eight?

Although born in 1963, I witnessed very few flower-child influences. One of my babysitters, Sharon, looked as though she had sprung from the Beatles' *Magical Mystery Tour*, and we used to spin that LP on my portable record player. We'd sing "Goo goo ga joob" until I fell down laughing. Sharon studied painting with my father, and some of his other students dressed in the fashion of '60s cool. One morning in our home on the Cape, for example, I almost stumbled into a fellow who looked a lot like Allen Ginsberg; he had crashed at our house for the night and, having risen with the sun, contorted his body in a mock headstand, his underpants aimed skyward towards enlightenment. I suspect many of these people smoked pot, but they never did so in our home because they knew my parents frowned on narcotics, even the mildest forms. I never became preachy about my aversion to drugs, but I was uninterested in grass and terrified of everything else.

That's partly why I find this episode so amusing: a painter of my father's generation had come to our house for dinner, and he brought his new wife, who was from India. I was fairly young but old enough to suspect this woman's "cigarettes"—to note that they were especially sleek, though I couldn't place the smell. My mother kept saying things like, "Don't those look interesting," trying to coax this woman into naming the drug, though I wonder how my mother would have responded to an admission: "Stop smoking right now, and please leave"? "I know you've had eight joints already, but I draw the line at nine"? Or, doubtful but possible, "When my son goes to bed, can I have a hit? I've never smoked before."

The woman repeated that she bought the cigarettes in India and that she much preferred them to American smokes, and my parents didn't say much more because, I guess, they didn't know how to admit their ignorance. During my travels many years later, I learned that these were, in fact, plain tobacco cigarettes from India, that they were perfectly legal and had absolutely no connection to marijuana. But it's significant that my parents and I didn't even know the smell of pot, and I still laugh when I think of my father at the end of that evening: picking up the ashtray filled with tiny stubs, emptying them into a baggie, and throwing the sealed contents into garbage cans, two blocks away from our house.

Although emotionally and physically removed from the world of drugs, I found myself captivated by stories of drug users, particularly artists I admired. Before I turned to jazz, the Beatles had been the soundtrack to my childhood, and learning that the song title "Lucy in the Sky with Diamonds" stood for LSD made me—age what? nine?—feel particularly hip. I loved the kaleidoscopic landscapes of that song: the sky glazed to marmalade, and this glowing woman dazzling the clouds. Newspaper taxis floated to the banks of *my* river, the Hudson. A headlined flap would fall open, and I'd be gone, Lucy would be gone, the song would be over, giving in to the pulse of "Getting Better." I could travel as far as I wanted, and wasn't that the point of the song? How could this be, exclusively, the effects of acid?

By the mid-1970s, when I focused absolutely on jazz, the realities of drugs had a more dramatic impact on my love of the arts, though the drug life remained just as much a fiction. Bizarrely, I enjoyed the stories about drug users, especially the one about Thelonious Monk trying LSD for the first time, how (according to myth) he had so many other drugs coursing through his system that he experienced no effect and responded with this dismissive evaluation: "Man, you gotta give me somethin' *stronger* than that!" I laughed every time I retold that anecdote, never once imagining the actuality of drugs and addiction.

I started to read more about jazz, but I'd read words like *junkie* and *addict* as casually as I read song titles. Then, in the winter of 1980, just two or three months after my mother's initial diagnosis, I came across Art Pepper's autobiography, ironically titled *Straight Life*, and it gave me a new perspective on the world of drugs. Never again could I relegate addiction to a purely historical frame of reference. Pepper brought me into a life I never wanted to see, forced me to experience—as best as any uninitiated young reader can—the devastating effects of narcotics. I remember particularly a passage depicting the year 1960, long after he'd established himself as a major voice on the alto saxophone and the same year that he recorded *Smack Up* and *Intensity*. His wife at the time, Diane, had already transformed from an innocent to an addict and had made at least one suicide attempt, locking the bathroom door and slicing both wrists. Pepper had done time (he'd do a lot more), and in the book he describes those days with unflinching detail. But it was this scene from 1960 that replayed in my mind:

> We went through an unbelievable scene in the little house we lived in, for four days, taking hundreds of pills. I remember I fell down over a table at one point and broke a lamp and cut myself. Diane would fall. It was a nightmare of falling on the

floor looking for pills. Diane had dropped the bottles and they broke. Diane was trying to get out of the house. Right near us was a wash, by Ventura Boulevard, with a big drain like a storm drain, and she wanted to go to this and she would have done it, but she couldn't get out the door. She couldn't find the door. She never found the door. I swear to God, she could not find the door.

Even in my saddest times, I've never known the depth of his or her desperation. If I've looked for doors, they've been entrances to possibilities, not an end—and I say that not with a sense of superiority but in gratitude for a childhood so opposite Pepper's. What life would he have lived had he been raised by a mother who learned to balance her love of family with a love of her craft? As if I needed such instruction, *Straight Life* taught me all I ever wanted to know about heroin and cocaine and amphetamines. I never criticized or condemned Pepper, or any of my heroes who found themselves lost in a landscape of drugs, but I embodied a primal fear of experimentation.

So it was a particularly surreal time when drugs began to control our home, though my father and I never discussed this, ever. Because it wasn't a matter of choice, ultimately: my mother's doctors thought marijuana would stimulate her poor appetite and that her relentless pain, too severe for that drug to alleviate, could be controlled with injections of morphine.

I learned about this proposed treatment from a social worker who'd been sent by an agency or the hospital—I'm not sure. She sat me down in the kitchen.

"I'm going to tell you something that you'll probably find shocking," she said.

"Okay."

"Are you relaxed? Because some people have a tough time dealing with this."

I thought to myself, *What could be more shocking than what we have now?* "Sure," I said.

"We'd like to medicate your mother with marijuana."

I nodded. She stared at me.

"Are you okay?" she asked.

"Yeah."

"Sure?"

"Yeah."

"Because some people have not handled this well. One girl lunged from a sofa and tried to choke me."

I could see that happening—I didn't care much for this woman—though I told her not to worry, and she said I was great, and I said it wasn't a big deal. Truth is, I wasn't angry at all and was, in fact, trying not to laugh, though I couldn't understand why I wanted to laugh. (Later, I thought of children who giggle when scolded, how we're naturally wired to release tension but can't always control the expression.) And then there was the word itself: *marijuana*. I couldn't recall anyone using the word in a serious sentence. *Grass*, yes. *Pot*, sure. *Weed*, *dope*, *joints*, even *reefer*. But *marijuana* sounded like a tropical resort, and she looked goofy overpronouncing each syllable.

Did she bring a small supply with her, or did my father retrieve some from the hospital? I don't remember, and I didn't witness my mother's first attempts to get high, if that's the appropriate phrase. Relatively soon, though, we ran out of the prescribed doses of pot (the social worker told us this would happen, that legal doses were minuscule) and had to find other sources. This turned out to be easy. We were in Manhattan. My father taught art. Many of his students, if they weren't smoking themselves, knew others who were. So each week, painting students donated bags of pot. It almost seemed like a competition: who could score the best shit.

Before the deluge of deliveries, however, we ran out of dope and had no backup plan; the buildup of marijuana in my mother's system had begun to have some effect—marginal, but noticeable—and, suddenly, we had no more medication and no legal resources. I knew my friend Karen could help us out because her mother smoked, but for a dismal hour I said nothing to my father, afraid that he'd forbid me to see Karen again. Then my mother's voice cracked our silence, and I nervously made the suggestion, and my father said: "Call your friend."

Karen's mother was very New York and had a range of therapists; later I referred to her as being "shrink-wrapped." And she knew about loss. Her greatest love—I think it was Karen's father, though I'm cloudy on that—had died unexpectedly, and her hottest lover had secretly carried on an affair with her other daughter, Karen's older sister. They had learned of this betrayal earlier that year, just a couple of weeks after they became a part of my life.

She told me to come over and I said I'd be there soon, since they lived only eight blocks away. I kept smiling, and chuckling. I couldn't wait to get there. I kept thinking: *You're going to buy pot.* Some of those blocks I walked, some I ran. When I rang their doorbell, Karen's mother answered the intercom with a puzzled tone; she couldn't believe I'd arrived so quickly.

That afternoon, I learned the basics: how to clean seeds and roll joints. She brought out cheap pot and expensive pot.

"Smell this," she said, placing a handful of dark hemp beneath my nose. "Earthy, right? That's what you want. The paper you use to roll—not so important. But you don't want too many seeds, and you want the pot to be good and earthy."

That's how I knew we had quality dope brought in by the students, and they would sit with me before class and help me roll joints for the week. I'd bring out my portable tape player. We listened to a lot of Mingus, especially the Ellington medley on *Mingus at Monterey* with Charles McPherson on alto, and for a while I thought McPherson's entry on "In a Sentimental Mood" was the most beautiful sound in the world. I'd practice that version of the tune on my own horn and could get the notes, even most of McPherson's tone, but it never sounded as awesome. I was no McPherson, and I didn't have the Charles Mingus trio behind me, and I never followed Mingus's fabulous bass solo on "I've Got It Bad and That Ain't Good." That's partly why McPherson sounded so dazzling: he followed the dark tones of Mingus in sweat, Mingus in shadow, Mingus all over that big bass until his music became mountains at midnight and the sun could rise in the golden bell of McPherson's horn.

Charles Mingus recorded *Mingus in Monterey* in late September 1964. It was his first appearance at the Monterey Jazz Festival, and the two-LP set from this date became the debut of his personally run record label: Charles Mingus Enterprises. Mingus relished the shift; for years he had felt cheated by the white establishment that controlled the distribution of his recordings. He could now sell this record on his own, primarily by mail order. For the first time in his life, he'd be in control of the music *and* the money.

The latest and largest biography on Mingus describes the Monterey concert this way: "He bowed a long, achingly lyrical solo take of Ellington's 'I've Got It Bad' . . . [and later, on 'Meditations'] dropped his bow and bobbed around the bass as he plucked thick, dissonant chords." But this is, at best, a reversed commentary. On "I've Got It Bad," the opening number, Mingus doesn't use his bow at all, and he's backed quietly by Dannie Richmond on drums and Jaki Byard on piano; "Meditations" begins with an almost classically structured bass solo—and Mingus uses a bow to achieve that sound. Mingus complained his whole career that critics didn't understand his music; decades after his death in 1979, even his advocates seem to fail him.

Like most jazz stories involving production and royalties, however, the distribution of *Mingus at Monterey* has neither a smooth history nor a happy ending. First of all, the recording's not without serious technical weaknesses. At times, the band surges with such ferocity that the engineers can't adjust, and some passages dissipate into a fuzzy hiss of distortion. But Mingus soon learned of the great and varied difficulties concerning record distribution. His problems culminated in a failed shipment to the following Monterey Jazz Festival, in 1965; instead of making a killing on sales, Mingus could only rant while thousands of copies of the double LP remained boxed in a warehouse. Certain that he had once again been intentionally screwed by the white superstructure of the recording industry, and by the director of the festival itself, Mingus pulled his orchestra from the bandstand after just one number.

In 1965 or '66, my father stopped by an art gallery in midtown Manhattan. He doesn't remember which one, nor does he recall the show itself; both have been eclipsed by his unexpected encounter with Charles Mingus, who sat behind a table and sold copies of *Mingus at Monterey*. "There was a nice, good-looking woman helping him out," my father told me, "and he kept railing against the record companies, explaining to anyone who listened that this record was *his* record." My father bought a copy and had it inscribed to our friend Thorpe, who, many years later, gave it to me.

That particular album, therefore, had a multilayered, deeply personal importance. At the time of my mother's illness, I yearned all the more for a personal connection to these legendary jazz figures, many of whom had already died, including Mingus. But I also turned to his music for its remarkable range of sound, which, in terms of emotion, seemed to me both true and instructive. What's more, I had just finished reading *Beneath the Underdog*, his now-famous autobiography that begins with a fabulous disclaimer: "Some names in this work have been changed and some of the characters and incidents are fictitious." (Unforgivably, Penguin cut the quote in its paperback reprint.) At sixteen, I focused primarily on the passages about sex—or was that the whole book?—and especially the advice from Buddy Collette's father about how best to make love to a woman. The description was so macho, so outrageously explicit and sexist. I must have read it forty times.

In the autobiography, Mingus writes surprisingly little about himself as a musician. I first read the book with no preconceptions and kept poring over the pages for detailed discussions of famous concerts, but I learned instead about wild, rather unbelievable relationships with women. Later, I read Brian Priestley's biography of Mingus, and the lovely memoir co-written by Al Young and Janet Coleman, and many articles on the great bassist. At the time, however, I gleaned biographical information from general reference books and from the liner notes to albums. That's what brought me to this passage by the bassist himself, printed on the back of *Mingus at Monterey*:

> I was playing to love and to the spirit of someone who lived somewhere on earth for me. A woman. When I'm in love, and I've been in love maybe twice, it seems as though I'm able to communicate with that person from miles away. I feel I can touch her if I concentrate or meditate or think of her.

It was this abstract woman that allowed his autobiography to make sense: in writing about passionate and passionless sex, and about the desperate need to find genuine love, Mingus *had* been talking about his music. I returned to his book and to his music with an understanding that had simultaneously become more abstract and concrete. *Maybe the whole world,* I thought to myself, *spins on the axis of desire.*

Because of my youth, and maybe because I was a first-generation American, I felt removed from Mingus's diatribes against white Americans. And I read with relief his aversion to drugs. Yes, Mingus remained dependent on a range of pills throughout his life, but he avoided more devastating narcotics. It's rumored that he tried snorting heroin once, that he kept away from it for the rest of his life because the drug made him sick, but we also know that Fats Navarro, the brilliant trumpeter and the bassist's close friend, frightened Mingus away from the "in" drug, and perhaps saved his life by doing so.

Navarro died at age twenty-six from complications of TB and smack, and Mingus had witnessed Navarro's meteoric decline: spitting blood and insisting, "I ain't afraid to die." Throughout *Beneath the Underdog*, Fats Navarro appears in conversation with Mingus, except that Navarro emerges as both teacher and student, not necessarily a heavenly guide to a supreme truth. "You don't listen, Fats," Mingus says.

> You're dying in your mind, killing yourself 'cause you want to. You don't go to bed five and six nights in a row. It's like talking to a man who has a razor at his jugular vein—I'm reaching out to stop him as the first gush of blood tells him he's on his way and he still doesn't realize it's his own hand with the razor.

Navarro responds:

> I do, Mingus. But I want to watch my enemies as I die and see their faces when they know they lost a steady client. I go out, kick my habit, come home clean. And right away there's some dirty motherfucker pulling on my arm to come and get high free this time 'cause he knows next I'll be knocking down his door to get in. Mingus, don't ever be no junkie. This world is a dirty place.

🎺

Maybe the darkness helped induce the drug's pull. Maybe it was out of shame. Whatever the reason, when my mother smoked, the light in her bedroom glowed barely more than a photographer's safety light. I grew accustomed to the smell of pot, but only one memory remains strong enough for me to recall the entire scene. My father has left for Philadelphia to teach for the night, and my mother has been joined by a close friend, who smokes at the foot of the bed but only as another form of comfort. (*Come—we'll do this together.*) Even in half light, I can still see—peripherally, because I want to watch but don't want my mother to catch me watching—the smoke swirl and mushroom.

"Try to hold it in your lungs a little longer," her friend says.

My mother takes a deep drag, but this induces a painfully common reaction: she begins to cough, then retch; she grabs for a disposable cardboard bowl and, her whole body twisted now in a near-convulsive response, spits up almost nothing. Finally, she leans back and makes a sound that translates to *I just can't.*

What was I doing on the floor of that room? It was much too dark to read, and I never listened to music there. Perhaps, with my father away, I felt more comfortable to witness this experience without his parental warnings or judgment. Perhaps it was pure curiosity, and the minor thrill of being enveloped by marijuana. I did not know at that time about contact highs, nor did I remain in the room long enough to feel the effects, because when my mother recovered from retching, she said, somewhat haltingly, "It's not so good, maybe, for you to be here . . ."

During those weeks when I rolled cigarettes for her, I never snuck one in my pocket for an illicit drag on the streets of Manhattan. I saw no joy in the act, and, in addition to respecting my rational and irrational phobias about marijuana, I never would have diminished her supply. This was medicine, and when my father's students and I rolled joints, we focused on the act itself. We carefully pinched our choice of dope and, every now and then, eyeballed the efforts by those around the kitchen table. We were serious, but not morbid, and I remember one night when the group became jocularly competitive:

"Mine's killer."

"No, no. Look at this one. This is what it should look like."

"Forget it," a third insisted. "You've made it too tight. You need a wider body, and a wider opening—you know, for an easy drag."

"But that's not classy. Look how sleek and uniform this is."

I didn't join in; I had no faith in my skills. Instead, I copied a bit from everybody and listened to the music, and that night we heard "Meditations" from *Mingus at Monterey*. Roughly twenty-five minutes long—warm-up through ovation—"Meditations" had originally been split in two parts (the end of side C to the start of side D) and I hated the break, so I spliced it together on a cassette tape using rudimentary equipment. Though crudely connected, the tape at least approximated the continuation of sound, and that was essential: "Meditations" *must* be heard without a break, for all the obvious reasons concerning the impact of live performance, the relentless drive of the arrangement, the push and pull of solo against solo, and the very nature of a meditation—especially this one, which had been inspired by the politics of race.

Thirteen minutes into that tune, Mingus and Byard play a duet, the bow twitching against bass strings as if he's actually cutting wires (in keeping with Mingus's concept for the composition, that of escape and freedom), and then Buddy Collette enters on flute. By the seventeen-minute mark, flute and bass actually speak—what they play becomes vocal—and two minutes later, Mingus slices his strings, and Richmond punishes his drum skins. Then the rest of the ensemble, some improvising and others working with minor orchestration, rumble in the background. Once again, the band surges out of the sound tech's capabilities, pedal to bass drum dropping out of the tape's memory. Twenty-two minutes now, and the tempo itself rises to a crisis for half a minute. Then the original theme for twenty seconds. Then silence. Blackout. It's over.

On record, you can almost hear the thousands of people stand. The applause lasts well over a minute.

In our kitchen, the competition over the best joint had ended early into the recorded performance. No one spoke, minute after minute, while Mingus's orchestra vibrated the wooden floor. During the ovation, a jubilant Mingus hugged his musicians, and when the clapping ceased, I turned the cassette player off.

"Jesus," one student said. "That was intense."

Then: "Yeah." And then they looked around the table. And then we placed all the joints collectively in the center of a rounded mahogany tray.

# Blouse Catching Smoke

At the very end of March, two weeks after the evening with Howard McGhee at the West End Jazz Café, I left New York City during my school's spring break to visit my oldest friend, Thorpe, and several other artists, people I'd known most of my life. In some respects, they were like older siblings: my parents, as teachers and confidantes, had become surrogate parents to a number of younger painters. This particular group had moved almost collectively to nearby areas on the north shore of Massachusetts. I knew my visit would be an important distraction from the pressures of home, but I never expected to fall in love.

The day I arrived, Thorpe told me that mutual friends, Bonnie and Ashley, had orchestrated a large gathering for the evening, one that included a number of old friends. As a joke, and only a joke, I asked if he could get me a date, and he took it seriously.

"I'll see what I can do," he said.

"Oh, I'm just kidding around."

"No, I'll see what I can do. I have someone in mind—she's at school. I'll see if she's free."

I'd never dated seriously and had never been set up before. Besides, he taught *college*. I figured this could only be a fiction and forgot entirely about our brief exchange. But that afternoon, while I stayed in his home and practiced my alto, Thorpe asked one of his students, Carol, whether she'd be willing to be my "escort." She wanted to know how old I was; he told her I was seventeen. Since she was twenty-two—five light-years older—his proposition didn't sound terribly appealing.

"Maybe," she said. "Can I leave it open?"

"Sure," he replied. "Of course."

At that moment, Carol had no intention of showing, and Thorpe could sense that. But later in the evening, her admiration for Thorpe as a teacher eclipsed her reservations about young-adult sitting, so she hopped into her rusting Pinto and drove the eight or nine miles to the party. No stranger to that crowd, she walked into the house and approached her teacher, who greeted her enthusiastically. I didn't know who she was, nor had I been told of their previous discussion, so I didn't fully understand Thorpe's glee. A minute later, he introduced us, and she sat down with me. I didn't speak to anyone else for several hours.

I could describe Carol by the blonde curls that framed her face, or the gentleness of her slender build, but more than any particular feature, it was her overall presence that seemed luminous. A family friend later described her as looking "like a Rembrandt," as if the light came from within, though that's somewhat misleading since photographs of her never capture that light. In professional portraits or casual snapshots, she looks washed out, her skin merely pale, but in person—even in the smoky haze of that dimly lit first floor—she inhabited a fairy-tale-like beauty.

At first, she talked to me out of obligation, and then something wonderful replaced duty: a pleasure in discussing the arts and the creative process. "Tell me," she said, "what it's like to play the saxophone, to breathe through a horn and make sound." No woman had asked me that (no high school junior had asked me *anything* about the arts), and I spoke to her with joy—joy and disbelief, the kind of bewildering pleasure that comes over you place when you witness, say, the landscapes of Arizona—when you become almost incapable of accepting the experience. I asked her about her paintings, said how much I'd love to see her work, and I meant it.

Throughout the house, the others quite happily talked and drank and laughed. Some argued; others provoked the arguments. Martinis and bourbon and beer bottles bopped to bop and post-bop. Dynamic abstract works, detailed pen-and-ink drawings, even mobile-like cutouts by children, reformed and energized the walls. All around us: a wild party of sound and silhouette. We were simultaneously in the center and miles away, huddled to the side with a large bottle of red wine that slowly stained our teeth and tinted the whole room to the essence of burgundy.

When the music stopped, I suggested that we choose some tunes and took her hand (I was proud of that). We walked through the living room and into the library, where the old KLM stereo, which had been spinning jazz records the whole afternoon while we prepared for the party and all night long as well, radiated heat. I pulled the stacked LPs from the turntable, and Carol, holding each record by the edges, slipped them into their covers.

"What shall we hear?" she asked.

"I'll take a look."

I was afraid she'd want to dance, because I knew nothing about dancing, and I didn't know how to tell her I knew nothing. I was still thoroughly astonished that she hadn't left my side, and I wanted to choose the right music. I almost couldn't make a selection, as if the wrong choice would send her away, and then my eye caught the white border of Dizzy Gillespie's *The Early Years*, with the famous side-view photo of Bird and Diz: Parker in a white jacket, formal as an alabaster sculpture; Gillespie on the right in a slight crouch, his trumpet—a straight horn, not one with his signature angle—firing at the back of Parker's skull. It's the record with "Salt Peanuts" and "Hot House," the one with young Sarah Vaughan singing "Lover Man." And as I pinched it from the shelf, Carol brought her hands around my waist, pulling me towards her as the LP's needle dropped into the record's groove, and we turned and turned across the room, our mouths open, until her shoulders reached the wall, and we slid to the floor, still kissing in a wilderness of jazz and wine.

༄

Because of my insecurity and inexperience, we did not make love that night. She knew I'd never been with a woman, and she was cool about it—uncaring about my past, and gentle about the present. But we did spend the night together, and sometimes I wonder whether I hurt her by holding her so tight.

In the morning, I tottered downstairs and saw several people from the party sitting around a card table and drinking Bloody Marys and screwdrivers to soothe their headaches and nausea. Later, I wondered where they had slept, but at that moment I had more immediate concerns.

"I couldn't sleep most of the night," I said. "The room kept spinning and my dreams seemed to be projected on a tilted screen—everything came to me at angles." I couldn't imagine why. "And now I've got this terrible headache."

"Aw, Christ," someone answered in a drawl. "Look—you've got a good old-fashioned hangover. Take two or three of these aspirins and go back to bed."

Then someone made an obvious joke, something like, "Yeah, I'm sure you've got a few more rounds in ya," and they laughed, and then someone else said, "Please don't make me laugh," and I staggered upstairs.

Carol had already dressed, and, feeling the effects herself, suggested we take a walk. She told me a bit about her past, and we talked more about painting. She knew my father had been Thorpe's teacher and, since she'd be graduating in a few weeks, she wanted to know about his classes, particularly the summer sessions on Cape Cod.

"Maybe I'll come to the Cape this summer," she said, and I leapt at the idea. I told her about our old barn where he taught, how she could stay at our home anytime she wanted, that people returned to those classes annually with an enthusiasm verging on religious fervor. I described the beaches and some restaurants, piano bars, and potteries. I babbled about any enticing detail that came to mind, and in doing so I told several stories about my childhood. But I didn't mention my mother's illness. I suppose it was a little like hearing Howard McGhee—that beautiful escapism and that near-desperate need to hold onto it. By the end of the walk, Carol seemed fully engaged by the idea of studying with my father. We said we would see each other again that night, and every night of my visit. She went home for a change of clothes, and I levitated back to the house.

When I walked in, however, I learned that my father had telephoned: I was to return immediately. Manhattan Transit Authority had threatened to strike, and he didn't want me to get stuck in Massachusetts. My joy curdled to a bitter anger, and I railed against the demand: "He can't *do* this. I don't *care* about any goddamn strike. It might not even happen, for Christ's sake. Why—is—he—*doing* this?" But even in my outrage, I knew I wouldn't win. "Please explain things to Carol," I said to Thorpe at the bus station, and then I thanked him, shook my head, and boarded the Greyhound for New York.

In those hours between Boston and Manhattan, my anger did not cool, nor did I even try to sympathize with my father—a husband who had witnessed a devastating change in his wife's health and who had used the transit strike as an excuse to get his son home quickly. Although my mother would stay alive for two more weeks, he didn't think she'd survive more than a couple of days and thought it would be a betrayal if I were not at home.

I figured this out almost as soon as I entered our house. The cancer had discovered new avenues, new ways of twisting the body. My mother's speech had become a slur of English and Swedish. She spoke half in a dream, conversing with her own father, who had died five years before. For the first time, I knew Death. He had walked through the walls when I left town, and now He had placed a palm within her jaw, his hand reaching towards the brain. It was beyond horrible—an experience balanced on that absolute yet indefinable line between horrible and unbearable.

The next morning, in a moment of lucidity, my mother said to me, "I'm so sorry. I've become so ugly," and I told her she hadn't, and she thought I was very sweet for lying.

On Monday, March 31, the day after I left Massachusetts, Carol wrote a letter that began, "I hope you've fully recovered from the past weekend's carousing. Or is such a thing possible?! And here I am, a ghost of the same, knocking on your door." She said she wanted to visit, but only if I wanted her to come, that she didn't want me to feel pressure. "I'll just tell you truthfully that you've been in my thoughts/feelings almost constantly since I saw you," she wrote. I replied that same day, thrilled by her words and sickened by the horrors at home that would keep us from seeing each other. "I don't know when my life will settle down," I wrote, having explained the circumstances, "but I will let you know as soon as I can."

In the third week of April, only a week after my mother died, I picked Carol up at Penn Station and brought her home. She was everything the house had not experienced for many months: beauty and happiness and vivacity. I took her to Riverside Park, its promenade lined with budding cherry trees, and we talked about music and painting, and about the hard year, though I didn't dwell on the subject. At one point, I showed her a subway grate, one I knew fairly well.

"No trains," I said, "but people go there to paint the walls."

She lay down on the iron and cupped her eyes to shield the sunlight—exactly the way I peered into those tunnels—and I just barely heard her as she said, "Yes, I can see the images now."

We went out to dinner with my father, who must have ached—I'm sure her beauty and creative spirit reminded him all too much of the wife he'd just lost—but he covered so well. Afterwards, he said he had things to do and left us alone upstairs, where we listened to jazz and kissed.

"I want to be with you tonight," I said to her.

"I want to be with you, too," she said.

"No—I mean, I want to make love."

She smiled, and then she looked meditative, sweetly serious, and she held my hand when she asked, "Are you sure?"

I'd never been surer of anything, but I could tell she had her own doubts, having slept only with older, more experienced men. Sometimes, when I think of that night and my impatient mind, I try to imagine what thoughts she must have had as she brushed her teeth and slipped into a nightgown. *Am I doing the right thing? Is this the right time?*

When she came to my side, I tentatively pulled her towards me. Very quietly, I started to speak: "I hope . . ." And then she placed three fingers over my mouth.

---

A few days later, she wrote to me about her ride home. "It was a nice thing," she said, "that just as I was leaving the city, I caught the very end of a reading from *Moby Dick*. It was a paragraph I'd written down just a month or so ago." Then she quoted the passage that concludes chapter 23, "The Lee Shore":

> Know ye, now, Bulkington? Glimpses do ye seem to see of that mortally intolerable truth; that all deep, earnest thinking is but the intrepid effort of the soul to keep the open independence of her sea; while the wildest winds of heaven and earth conspire to cast her on the treacherous, slavish shore?
>
> But as in landlessness alone resides the highest truth, shoreless, indefinite as God—so, better is it to perish in that howling infinite, than be ingloriously dashed upon the lee, even if that were safety! For worm-like, then, oh! who would craven crawl to land! Terrors of the terrible! is all this agony so vain? Take heart, take heart, O Bulkington! Bear thee grimly, demigod! Up from the spray of thy ocean-perishing—straight up, leaps thy apotheosis!

My schoolmates were dating young women whose greatest crises revolved around the labels on their jeans, and I—I had fallen in love with a woman in her twenties. Who knew Melville. Who would quote from great works of literature because the texts became a living commentary on our lives. Who would share that joy in a letter because it could become another avenue to understanding each other.

Except that's not at all what went through my mind. I had not read *Moby Dick*, nor did I understand the quoted passage, and I didn't try. Why write about this Bulkington when she could write about *us*? I had discovered sex; my apotheosis was leaping, all right, and I didn't care about any other guy, especially not a fictitious one. What was she thinking?

I never, in fact, resolved my confusion over what I felt were two separate selves: the Carol I knew in person, giving herself fully to the urgency of the present, and the voice of her letters, which seemed distracted, if not emotionally removed. Going back to her correspondence, I'm amazed at how little I understood her—the obvious confusion that permeated almost every paragraph, how she was working through all sorts of issues regarding professional and personal goals. I was a long year away from graduating high school, and she was graduating art school, fully in the process of discovering herself as an artist.

I loved every visit, but we very naturally followed our own paths, and by the time I went to college, we were definitely not a couple. We'd broken up without breaking up, and without any regret. Our relationship, in fact, ended better than any other, and I never thought of Carol as the great love that I lost; the only woman I ever wanted to marry, I married. But years later, I wrote a poem that clearly had its roots in autobiography—taking place at a party much like the one where I first met Carol—and maybe, in the last three stanzas, I was offering a good-bye that had been, for the most part, unspoken:

> Driving alone to Thelonious's septet,
> I often wonder if she ever made it
> South, summer in New Orleans, her paisley
> blouse catching smoke, blues bands
>
> outside the French Quarter:
> shadows of trombone slides and clarinets
> muting their solos across her eyes.
> Before she drove away, I held her
>
> close enough to feel against my face
> her hair, curling and smelling
> sweet, almost like the vapors
> of whiskey, almost like cedar.

There's the suggestion that traveling to the South had been this woman's dream—and it was not, as far as I knew, Carol's. (Many details in the poem shape-shifted in order to make it a more complete work.) But that is, in fact, where Carol ended up traveling: through the Carolinas, into Louisiana, and, finally, to Mexico. She made this trip with a boyfriend who had introduced her to vintage motorcycles, of all things. In races, she'd ride the sidecar, her skull at every quick turn just inches from the track.

I know this for all the worst reasons, and maybe I should end the story before that trip to Mexico in 1998, when she walked by herself along a popular beach in Puerto Escondido while her boyfriend stayed at the resort to work on a bike. That's when two men assaulted her: a local construction worker who had previously been arrested for raping a tourist, and his friend, described in national newspapers as "a drifter." They beat her, leaving deep marks in her back, and raped her, and then they threw her, still alive, into the shallows, where she drowned.

For months, the Mexican authorities claimed there wasn't enough evidence for an arrest, but Carol's sister and parents bulldoggedly pursued justice, and as a result, Carol's murder became known nationally. All the major newspapers carried her story, and then I began to see her on television: a two-part program for *20/20*, a feature on NBC's *Today Show*. Hugh Downs and Barbara Walters mouthing warnings to America. Carol's sister and brother-in-law pleading for justice, and then her pixilated face.

Last I heard, the two men lost their final appeal and will serve forty years each. There have been, apparently, many memorial services in her hometown, as well as at Yale, where she received a master's degree in painting, and elsewhere. Her family has created a Web site in her honor, with a toolbar that navigates her life: Home, Site Map, Carol, Art Center, Tragedy, Memorial, News. People were encouraged to post their reflections, and it's clear that about a third of these writers never actually knew her; they followed reports in the media and cast their thoughts onto the World Wide Web, our twenty-first-century

Atlantic: "Glimpses do ye seem to see of that mortally intolerable truth."

For years, Carol had been quite beautifully a part of the past. But the thought of her dying that way consumed me. As if in a low-flying glider, I kept hovering over her body, half-floating in the shallows of Escondido. I knew the men had used their teeth and their boots. Quoting Melville, she had written, "better is it to perish in that howling infinite, than be ingloriously dashed upon the lee." At what point during the attack did she realize, "I will not survive this"?

And how to grieve? At home, even on the day I learned of her death, I tried to pretend she wasn't on my mind, although I told my wife shortly after I heard the news, and I'm sure she knew better. Later that afternoon, my son asked if I would play Wiffleball in the backyard. I tossed a few pitches until he connected, and the white ball whirred overhead while I stared at a massive beehive in our hedge, thinking about the evening when I'd soak the hornets' entrance with lighter fluid or some poisonous, foaming spray. If I could gently pull the branches aside, I might even be able to save the hive and show my son its papery perfection. I knew he'd never seen the inside of a nest before, and I didn't think it was a shame to kill the hornets. "Fuck them," I thought. "What good do they do in this world?"

And then my son, who must have rolled his eyes at his father's disconnection from the planet, yelled, "Get the ball, Dad . . . Dad! Are you playing or not?" And then I heard my wife's voice from behind the screen door: "Come in, guys. It's getting dark."

# Where We Sleep

Perhaps exaggeration is the only way to be true to this memory. The accurate height of the doors is six feet. But when I'd think of them, and I thought of them often, they grew to ten or fifteen or twenty feet. I would see the doors from the bottom, not quite like Gulliver at Brobdingnag, but most certainly from the perspective of someone fully dwarfed. The doors had been pulled tight—my mother had died an hour earlier—and my mind kept refilming the sealed entrance, a large expanse of oak, because I wouldn't open those doors. For years, I felt I had failed my mother by not acknowledging her corpse.

Although there must have been countless times when the doors had been shut this way, I can recall only one other instance: the afternoon of the hypnotist, a man my father hired to teach my mother how to escape pain. The event failed, and, during the whole year of my mother's illness, this was the only time I remember her speaking angrily: she could hear us walking up the stairs and on the floorboards above, she said, and she could not lose herself in the experience. It made me unusually defensive and my father unusually apologetic. He promised her we would all be more attentive next time, though the hypnotist never returned.

Even now, when those bedroom doors close, the whole first floor of the brownstone redefines itself and makes me claustrophobic. It's not that I need to see into the bedroom, but I need to know that the space is there—or is it simply associative terror? Whatever the cause, when I saw the doors shut, I often walked upstairs to the living room on the second floor, a room I knew better than any other, for during my last two years of high school, that's where I slept.

This was my third "bedroom," though the moves didn't bother me. To some degree, the whole house felt like everybody's room: I spent most of my youth playing on the floor of my parents' bedroom, we ate dinners in the kitchen, my mother's studio was also our guest room, we had no master bath, the basement was an art studio used for teaching, and so on. When I see modern floor plans for housing, I still find it odd that every room has been predefined and compartmentalized absolutely.

We moved to the brownstone in 1965, following two years of shuttling around in downtown New York. (Landlords sold the properties, and the lofts where my parents lived in the early 1960s have been leveled and paved over for parking lots.) My father paid a laughably small amount for the house, yet he still thought he had made the biggest mistake of his life; he kept obsessing over possible parallels with Rembrandt, who never recovered, financially, from real-estate burdens. But my father was fifty, with a thirty-three-year-old wife and a two-year-old son, and he had experienced enough anxiety over temporary housing.

Both parents missed the huge, single-room expanse of the old lofts, but the brownstone's high ceilings approximated the space they knew and needed. On the first level, for example, a large kitchen space sweeps into a hallway (with a door to the cellar on the left, a bathroom and closet to the right), then the double oak doors open to a still-larger space that became their bedroom. Against the far wall, French doors front a small courtyard, and off that same wall, jutting into the yard, is a windowless room that had probably been a walk-in closet, or perhaps a bathroom. (The shower and bath on the second floor rest directly above and the spaces share identical dimensions.)

Whatever its original purpose, this room became my room, and I slept there for about thirteen years—until the age of fifteen.

I rarely invited classmates home from school, but the few who visited invariably laughed when they saw my room. They couldn't get over the size, couldn't imagine themselves limited to such a space. "I have too much stuff," they'd say. "Don't you want more stuff?" But I actually *liked* the compactness. Besides, I had more storage space than they realized; when I turned seven or eight, my father placed my bed on top of dressers he'd salvaged from the street—L-shaped: one at the end, two on the side—so that the setup approximated a bunk bed. I had drawers full of Legos and excellent books. I felt deprived of nothing. I simply could not comprehend why anyone would be bothered by a small sleeping space.

Then my mother urged me to share her art studio on the second floor, a large room with a high ceiling, and one with a queen-sized guest bed. The move seemed strange to me at first, since I had slept in that other room for so long, but by then I was listening more seriously to music, and playing my saxophones, and I was typing a good deal (papers, letters, stories), so I agreed. And I soon learned that I welcomed space and light, and that it had been a little weird to have slept in that small room for so many years. The revelation somewhat paralleled my introduction to jazz: I hadn't been unhappy with the music I knew, but this was so much better.

Still, I never called the new space "my room." I'd say, "This is where I sleep," or, "My mother paints here during the day and I crash here during the night." Furthermore, the arrangement didn't last long. Shortly after my mother's diagnosis, we telephoned her mother in Sweden, and when my grandmother arrived, I gave her that room. No other option would have made sense.

At that point, I slept on the sofa in the upstairs living room, and I enjoyed it there. The sofa itself did not pull out into a bed but had a long removable cushion for its back. In winter, the radiators in the adjacent brownstone warmed our walls as well, and when I curled on my side, I could place the soles of my feet against the hot, smooth plaster. When I visit the house now, I don't even sit on the sofa. (The springs gave way years ago, and although my father frequently "repaired" the seat with plywood and God-knows-what, it's genuinely uncomfortable.) But for those last two years of high school, I thought I had lucked into the most marvelous bed in the world.

Of all the rooms in the brownstone, that living room with the sofa has remained most true to my childhood images of the house, and it's the only one that affords spaciousness. The twelve-foot ceilings seem even taller, and the walls have not moved in the way they have throughout the house, although the room has always been decorated with a variety of delightful, if not unique, art and artifacts. In front of the sofa, for example, my father made a six-foot table from a mapmaker's board—you can still see the pin holes in the wood—that he found on the street. (It's half of a twelve-foot piece; my father stored its identical companion somewhere in the house, though I don't know where and have never seen it.) The chairs and love seats surrounding the table were also found items, most from the streets of New York, with one round-backed chestnut chair hailing from a beach on Cape Cod. My father used to reglue the loose arms, and my mother roped the seats and sewed cushions; in at least one case, she reupholstered the entire chair.

In one corner, my mother's weavings hang behind her large loom, and paintings by both parents warm the other walls. But I think most people remember the panoply of objects that turn the room into a sculpture. This truly is a *living* room. Here's some of what is immediately visible: a wooden case, with brass studs, constructed to ship a cello and looking like a medieval torture chamber; a seven-foot bamboo fishing trap from Indonesia; nestling steamed-rice baskets; two iron sculptures by Jeff Schiller that seem simultaneously filled with motion and indescribably dense; a floor-standing candelabra as well as candles of assorted colors and sizes in various locations; an open wooden chest overstuffed with yarn; a floor-to-ceiling bookshelf with art books wedged vertically, horizontally, even at angles, to maximize the space; curving boards carved by Wharton Esherick; some small drawings, copper reliefs, and soapstone sculptures that I made as a kid; bulbous glass jars and iron cauldrons; masks, icons, antique tools; a bureau of LPs; a rolltop desk with tiny, velvet-lined drawers; parquet flooring, mainly covered by discarded Persian rugs;

and a Mexican clay pig and an African cow head with a stiff tongue curling off the edge of a long shelf.

Then, and now, each object defined itself by not defining itself. Collectively, they seemed woven together by plants and driftwood and, even more so, by the overall sense that everything belonged together. At night, the room glowed from the light of an oval Noguchi lamp near the loom, and from a clay lampshade that my mother made, and from the street, since one wall is almost entirely composed of narrow windows. I liked the shadows from those street lamps, how they diffused through the curtain sheers, transforming hanging plants and sculptures and glassware. Even against the most despairing sounds from the floor below, I would follow form to form as if they were constellations in the night sky of sleep.

But I slept poorly. Brief hours, and for most of the time I felt aware of my sleep, drifting more consciously than unconsciously as if my mind safeguarded itself. When I did manage to sleep deeply, I often woke in a panic. Soon, I felt controlled by the night.

So I began a dream journal, and although the act of writing did not diminish the intensity of my dreams or the superficial quality of sleep, I felt more empowered and at ease. Like most people, I had to jot down central images immediately or they'd be gone by morning, but it didn't take a great deal to recover the whole dream, just a line or two: black dogs in the subway; a trembling square box of soil; a wire-cage elevator. Mainly, I recovered nightmares. But I had at least two wondrous dreams, both involving journey and water, and, to this day, the imagery returns with the clarity of profound personal experience.

In the first, I'm walking on a beach that's so fogged in that I can barely see my own footprints. The sky and ocean blur to a mist; it's all a haze, except that the clouds of mist keep rising and reshaping to approximate a path I can follow. I do not feel lost or frightened. Then I look down and find a piece of ice about the size of a fist. It's cubed, and when I pick it up, I see in each panel a magnificent face that, with no uncertainty, I recognize as the head of Neptune.

In the other dream, I'm swimming in the ocean, very deep in the water but without the need for any breathing apparatus. Even farther below, I see a spot of brilliance, and as I swim closer, the color from within this blue-black depth widens. Then it's all in focus: orange and red eels, each four or five feet long, slowly swirling until I'm so much in the center of these colors that I am actually part of the flamelike radiance—that there is not, in fact, a center or an end.

I now see these dreams as personal guides towards serenity: within the most devastating, opaque experience exists an all-consuming spirituality, one that many people seek in organized religions and that others find in the creative arts. At the time of those dreams, my sense of comfort was tangible yet inexplicable. For reasons alien to my consciousness, I had walked with Poseidon, and traveled to His world, a world not unlike the dreamscape of imagery in the living room where I slept.

Early into my mother's illness, she learned that one of her closest friends, Pat, had smashed into an oncoming car, headlight to headlight. Given the extent of the damage, it's remarkable that no one died or was paralyzed. But Pat suffered. (I won't chronicle the injuries; it's more than enough to note that surgeons extracted teeth from her nasal cavities.) When she had healed enough to speak, she telephoned. I think that's when she admitted she'd fallen asleep at the wheel. Her daughter had also been asleep, curled in the foot area in front of the passenger seat; she woke to witness what the accident had done to her mother—the endless amounts of blood—but by the next morning, she had repressed all memory of the event. I remember my mother's half of the telephone conversation, how she kept saying, almost like a chant, "Oh, Pat . . . Oh, Pat . . ."

What an excruciating time this must have been for Pat, and on so many levels: the guilt, the pain, the minute improvements during rigorous physical therapy—all the time thinking, "I'm not there for my best friend. She's dying, and I can't be with her." And how many times each day did she refilm the sequence of that late-night drive? Could she remember the moment when her eyes began to close?

By the time she had healed well enough to visit, my mother had lost so much identity, and Pat could neither reclaim those months nor offer much comfort. Like everyone else, she acted almost exclusively as a witness, and that helplessness fueled a desire to save someone—anyone. Returning to our house one afternoon, she saw a woman shivering on the corner. The woman called herself Rosie, and she never stopped trembling, her lips twisting and outlined in a near-neon pink. Perhaps she was a homeless junkie, or a homeless prostitute, but she most certainly was homeless. Detached from sensibility, Pat brought Rosie into our house and started making calls for shelters.

Rosie had no intention of going to the shelters. It was chilly outside, and she seemed grateful to be warm. But at one point she became increasingly agitated, as if she wanted to say, "Thanks for the couple of hours. Now let me go." And Pat wouldn't do it; she kept stalling. Then she offered to accompany her to the shelter, but Rosie insisted she knew how to get there. Eventually, she went out into the night. I'd see her on the street every now and then, but we didn't have much to say to each other. Maybe we nodded.

Rosie's visit took place five or six years before the homeless began to make their city-within-a-city along the Amtrak rails in Riverside Park, a covered stretch of track between 72nd Street and 123rd. I knew the rails existed because I walked the park many times each week, heading south from 90th. These were my stomping grounds: pickup baseball games, the Soldiers and Sailors Monument just a block away. As a kid, I'd lie on the grates long enough for my eyes to adjust, the smell of train tracks strangely attractive, until the iron and gravel began to take shape. But I never witnessed, nor did I ever imagine, the formation of a community.

Built in 1850, the railway followed the Hudson River's shore, and in the 1930s, when the city decided to extend the park, they built an enormous steel enclosure, later covered in earth to create, in effect, a long tunnel that runs parallel to the West Side Highway. For a while, the city used the line exclusively for freight cars, but then abandoned altogether the miles of ventilated track, as well as a series of large, concrete cubicles built for workers and electrical equipment. In those rooms, and elsewhere, scores of people created homes beneath my home.

Bernard Isaac, known during his stay as "King of the Tunnels," claims to have established this community in 1985, that he was first to occupy the rooms and that everyone else followed his lead. That's close to the truth, but at least two people set up housing in 1974, and countless others visited those tracks on a weekly basis. I know this because of the spray painting seen from above, the tag names and dripping images that I'd squint to find while lying across the park grates. And if I was underground, heading downtown on the IRT from 96th, I'd always watch for the 91st Street ghost station—abandoned in 1959—with its ever-changing murals. But from either location, above or below, I never saw a single graffiti artist or homeless person.

Nor did I make any effort to find their entrances. I had observed enough along the more remote areas of Riverside Park to fear the underground. (I'm thinking now of a walk during which I almost stepped on chicken claws and a hoof set beside a charred brass medallion and bits of charcoal.) Sometimes I peered through the stone archway off 95th, an entrance grated top to bottom and framing a padlocked door. I could see a metal landing and steps descending to the tracks. I don't think I tested the locks, or the iron spokes, but I know now that they loosened over the years, because this became the front door for Bernard Isaac and the many who followed.

In Margaret Morton's *The Tunnel*, Bernard describes his bedroom this way:

> I had two big Persian rugs. They were about 5 x 10 feet. And the furnishings were a bed, a dresser. I just had wicker furniture. It was bad. Was very comfortable. Was like, when you got in there and you looked and you say, "Wow! I can't believe this is where a homeless person was set up." . . . You could be livin' as comfortable as you chose. You could be as fabulous, as elaborate as you wanted it to be. Depends about how much time you want to put into it because the furnishings are unlimited out here on the streets.

Morton's stark photographs, however, make the room seem far less inviting. Bernard's bed is a mattress. His chairs look like public school rejects (nothing's wicker). The floor's mainly bare. It's not to say he lied; it's just that the words don't mesh with the images.

And maybe people stole his belongings. "I never was bothered, really," explains a former tunnel dweller named John, "until I started decorating my house. People didn't like the idea because I was outdoing everybody, and I was supposed to be a big shot and this and that." In Morton's photo of John's bedroom, silver Christmas streamers with flying doves and baubles loop from iron girders. Various drawings checker the painted cinder-block walls. He's placed stuffed animals on the bed and in the corner. From afar, the stacked milk crates look empty, but they act as a platform for a sculpture of a lion. John estimated "owning" about twenty-five cats, and five of them appear in the bottom right of the photograph; perhaps he's bringing food, because they're fixed on the same object, all staring at an angle to the lens. It's the most residential portrait in the collection, but even this is unmistakably the home of the homeless.

In articles from the *New York Times* and in books such as *The Tunnel*, John's life has been followed with some care. Like many others, he ended up in government housing when Amtrak resumed service on the lines. Endorsed by Mayor Giuliani, authorities plowed under the plywood homes built at the south end of the tunnel and then padlocked and soldered the primary entrances on the Upper West Side. This appears to have worked. The last time I visited Bernard's former entrance, just a few blocks from my former bedroom with its compilation of art and found objects, the snow that had fallen days before remained untouched. Not a footprint anywhere nearby—just a graying layer of speckled soot from the West Side Highway.

At two in the morning on April 15, 1980, I woke to the static of police radios. In less than a minute, I realized that the sounds emanated from the kitchen, and I knew what that meant. I waited to hear the front door close, then walked downstairs.

"She's gone," my father said.

"I know."

"You'll want to go in now—if you want to go in. They'll be taking her away soon."

"No," I said. "That's okay."

"Are you sure? They're coming soon."

"Yeah. I'm sure."

My father said he wanted to borrow my Polaroid camera to take some final photographs. I found it upstairs, returned, and handed it to him. Then he walked off, and I heard those large oak doors crackle open like a vault, and I turned towards the bedroom just as the camera flooded the dark interior with a nuclear bloom: *Flash*; electric *zip* of ejected film.

A moment later, my father said, "I can't get this to focus," his voice more edgy as he reached the last word in the sentence. *Flash*. "Can't you do this?"

But I refused. "It's autofocus," I said. "It should work by itself."

*Flash*. I wondered who would come for the body: more police, or maybe people from the crematorium. I wondered, too, if my grandmother was awake and if she had simply decided to stay by herself for these hours.

"No," my father yelled, "I can't get it to focus." *Flash; flash; flash*.

I forget how many years passed before I saw those Polaroids. At first, I didn't even know what had been captured, what I was seeing. My father never managed to focus the camera because he kept holding the lens too close to her face—so near that the autofocus could not adjust—and so her features became distorted even more than they already had naturally: a surreal death mask, with bleached colors spreading like oil paints.

And for a long time, the image of those doors—sealed, then flashing, then sealed again—kept pressing into my memory as if they were the entryway to a house of guilt, but I didn't tell anyone about this until I was a junior or senior in college. It must have been a holiday, because I was in New York City visiting my father, and I went out to lunch with the woman who had been closest to my mother during that final year. We ate at a Chinese restaurant—I remember that, because I kept staring at the orange koi and wondering how the employees kept the tank so clean. The glass had absolutely no algae, and the water was clearer than water.

I didn't tell her about the Polaroids, but at one point I admitted being plagued by guilt. I made myself say it: "I've always felt so terrible about not going into the room."

She stopped eating. "My God," she said. "Anita wouldn't have *wanted* you in the room."

I don't think an obvious truth has ever stunned or liberated me more. Even my despairing feelings about failing my father—Why couldn't I have helped him with the camera?—seemed to be physically pushed from my soul by a larger, more spiritual obligation.

Then a waiter brought to the adjacent table a deep-fried sea bass garnished with ginger and sprigs of spring onion. The couple ate quickly but carefully, finding the sweet flesh in the cheeks of the fish. Thinking of them now in that glassed-in restaurant on the Upper West Side, I'm reminded how beautiful a restaurant can be: strangers brought together in a room that, for the duration of a meal, anyone can call his own.

# Thelonious Maximus

The poetry of Charles Olson and Ezra Pound used to bewilder and intrigue me, and I always opened their books when I came across them in our home because their poems pushed from the page, as if they were word paintings. Like jazz, which I appreciated only years later in terms of theme and technique, sense and structure, these modernist poems captivated my interest for abstract reasons that I could not articulate. They simultaneously confused and liberated my sense of language. If I understood an image or a reference, fine. But I didn't feel particularly troubled or dumb if I didn't comprehend the narrative; I just loved watching the words fall.

Even today, I can imagine the pages of Pound's *Cantos* and Olson's *Maximus Poems* without recalling particular lines and cannot, in fact, remember which poems I encountered. But one afternoon, when I was about fifteen, I opened a collection by William Carlos Williams, whose work I did not know, and I can tell you quite exactly what I read because, to my astonishment, Williams invoked painters whom I admired:

>                The neat figures of
>                          Paul Klee
>                                    fill the canvas
>           but that
>                          is not the work
>                                    of a child   .
>           the cure began, perhaps
>                          with the abstraction
>                                    of Arabic art
>           Dürer
>                          with his *Melancholy*
>                                    was aware of it—
>           the shattered masonry. Leonardo
>                          saw it,
>                                    the obsession,
>           and ridiculed it
>                          in *La Gioconda*.
>                                    Bosch's
>           congeries of tortured souls and devils
>                          who prey on them
>                                    fish
>           swallowing
>                          their own entrails

Williams published these lines in *Paterson V* (1958), and, roughly twenty years later, they locked into the spirit of my adolescence: great enthusiasm inspired by the energy of other arts. (How Williams would have liked this story!) Klee could be common ground. Bosch could be redrawn with words so as to make something *else*. It was the first time I realized that poetry could wrap its arms around the visual arts and that language could invoke the spirit of music, too; indented by the tabs on Williams's typewriter, the lines lapped rhythmically. On its own, flush left, "swallowing" began to swallow itself, and the fattened period floating at the line's unending end delighted my eyes.

By my junior year, I owned a copy of *Paterson* and often brought

Williams's *Selected Poems* to high school so that I could read his work during lunch. I appreciated my eleventh-grade English class on British authors, and my teacher, even if his delivery came across like a bare ruined choir. But nothing we read resonated with the enthusiasm of Williams. I'm not sure whether we even read any writers from the twentieth century. Those who come to mind are Arnold, Browning, Tennyson, and Hopkins—definitely Hopkins, because every student received an oral report assignment, and I had to discuss his famous sonnet "Felix Randall," written in 1880, three years before Williams was born and exactly a hundred in the past.

Poor Felix Randall. In fourteen lines, we learn that this Superman-of-a-blacksmith—able to shoe tall stallions in a single pound—sickened until "Sickness broke him," and he died. He'll never again enjoy the "boisterous years." But I had no emotional response to this elegy.

The morning of my report, my teacher brought me into the hallway to apologize. "I handed out the assignments randomly," he said. "I didn't realize that this poem would be such a terrible choice."

I looked at him blankly and asked, "What do you mean?"

"Well . . ." He hesitated. "What with all that's happening at your home—this was probably the last poem you wanted to discuss."

Why wasn't he right? How is it possible that I didn't connect my mother's illness with the elegy? I had no answers, told my teacher not to be concerned about it, and gave a perfectly fine, passionless explication of the poem.

I've come to realize the obvious, that I distanced myself from personal experience mainly out of a need for emotional preservation, and out of a lack of interest: no British writer from previous centuries connected me to what might be termed a jazz aesthetic. Hopkins improvised with language, yes, and I appreciated Hopkins much more than most others from that course (and *so* much more now). But he sounded nothing like Williams, or Pound or Olson, for that matter. I wanted literature to be in the American grain and compared everything in my life to the wonders of jazz. Against the piano solos of Thelonious Monk, everything I studied seemed tame as hell.

Had anyone asked just a few weeks ago what other courses I took during my junior year, I would have shaken my head and offered a goofy smile, but I can answer that now, thanks to my father, who saved numerous report cards, including one from the end of that year. The report compiled individual pages for each course, and most were dated April 11, 1980—four days before my mother died. The cover note from the head of the school stated that I had "done very well during a difficult time," but my grades were nothing special. My music teachers (one for jazz ensemble, one for AP music theory) offered enthusiastic, one-sentence responses to my work; those were my only As. I got a B in biology and a B-minus in trigonometry; "Sascha's work this quarter," my math teacher noted with unremarkable insight, "has been rather inconsistent." My Spanish teacher—a favorite at that time and later, heartbreakingly, the faculty advisor for the Young Republicans—gave me a B-plus. *No está mal por un gringo.*

And I got a B-plus in "British Authors," which was higher than I deserved. "Sascha continues to keep abreast of his work more effectively than I can reasonably expect in view of the emotional stress he is under," my teacher said. "He wrote an excellent free composition at the beginning of the semester—a composition that was both perceptive and complex in its handling of emotions. His analytical papers have not explored their subjects quite as fully as did his earlier papers, and it is understandable that the required concentration should be a little lacking."

That my analytical skills had fallen below par had little to do with dramatic distractions at home and more to do with the skills themselves: it took another year before I fully understood the complexities inherent in expository prose. But what "free composition" had I written that induced such a kind response? I sifted through the photos and report cards, the poor analytical essays and the science projects. Nothing. I weeded through school bills and parental notices that had found their way into the same boxes. I looked hard, and as I did so—long before I actually uncovered the piece—the story began to emerge from complete erasure.

Quite predictably, my narrator reflected my self absolutely (a boy my age whose mother was dying of cancer), though I sketched that information in the briefest of ways. Most of the story takes place in a fictitious one-room shop on Amsterdam Avenue. The woman running the store starts to talk to me about her family, because she lost just about everybody in the Second World War. In the middle of the room, heated by an unseen radiator and near several cats curled in cushioned chairs, she shares photographs of the dead, and when she's through, she gives me a book on Sweden and refuses payment. I step out into the cold Manhattan air, and for the first time I notice the berries on the vine climbing the church adjacent to her building, how they tremble in the wind almost exactly like the ones that cover my home.

I see that story now as the start of my life as a writer, the moment when I understood the power of metaphor—even if the metaphors now seem painfully obvious—and the impact of simple but true dialogue. For Williams, that moment arrived when he wrote about rain driving the clouds, a meteorological inaccuracy (he knew that even then) but, nevertheless, a thrilling, liberating image for him. For me, the exchange with that woman warmed my whole being, and I can still feel the pressure of my Smith Corona typewriter keys clicking a steady rhythm against the unsteady melodies of our house as I typed and retyped those pages, not fleshing out a plot line but allowing the fictional experience to work through me. Up until that point, I had lost myself only in the act of making music, and now, from that same place within, came this story.

Had I not been playing so much music, I would have written much more—I'm fairly confident about that—though most of what I've unearthed from that time, primarily explications and academic exercises, bores and embarrasses me. In the box with my high school report cards, however, I also came across an oversized notebook given to me by a favorite English teacher. Inside, she inscribed these words, written not as a poem but with dashes and line breaks that approximated the dance of modern poetry:

> to Sascha: —
>     Not a blank page but
> rather a confidant—trust
> it—give to it—

>                    from one who knows the
>           comfort of a blank page—
>                          Much love and respect—
>                                 Always
>                                    Jane

That inscription is dated April 7, 1980, just a week before my mother died, but my first entry doesn't appear until two months later, on June 9, and the first fourteen pages have nothing to do with tragedy. Instead, I describe a trip that the school took to Toronto for a series of concerts. I was a leader in the jazz ensemble and a minor voice in the chorus. Both groups attended. We played well, behaved outrageously off the stand, wore out our teachers (who never again chaperoned a bus tour), and had a magnificent time.

I made the last Toronto entry on June 12. Two days later, I left with my father to spend the summer on Cape Cod, and I didn't write again in the journal until Saturday, June 17. "I'm not sure if I fully accept the fact that I have lost a mother," I wrote in the second paragraph. "It's also strange to be able to enjoy myself—to be able to take long bike rides and not have to worry about school or home or anything." The next day's entry is only half a page. For the first time, I acknowledge that I have "blocked out" my mother's past completely: "My mind refuses to look back on it in fear that I will be hurt again." I mention the comfort of music, the need for friends. I talk about the weather. But the prose, it seems to me now, becomes more and more self-conscious, as if I'm writing for somebody else and not giving myself to the page, the way I most certainly did with my story, and the way Jane had suggested. The last paragraph concludes with this trite observation: "Nothing in this world is permanent."

The remaining 150 pages are blank.

I initially opened Charles Olson's *Maximus Poems* not because I loved poetry but because I loved my friend Thorpe, who had actually known Olson; I had heard the poet's name long before I knew his work. In 1956, after the closing of Black Mountain College, Olson moved to Gloucester, Massachusetts, and lived in a second-floor apartment, retaining the place even after his wife, Betty, died in a car accident in 1964. (Olson died in 1970.) I visited that apartment on December 17, 1971. I was eight, and Thorpe was getting married—in the apartment itself—to a fine poet named Linda who had lived there as Olson's housekeeper. She'd left Gloucester for several months after Olson died, but then returned and rented the place herself.

This was a great, funky apartment, with a series of windows that afforded spectacular views and poor insulation. Both came into play that day, and the next, when a storm hit Gloucester and liberally blew snow beneath the front door. (I also remember the refrigerator door coming off when my mother opened it. "Watch your feet," Linda said.) But more than the subsequent storm, I recall looking out into the sunny, serene afternoon and noticing the wedding rings on the window sill. Venus, Linda explained to me, could be visible at twilight, its color changing with the evening, and Mars and Saturn could also be seen early in the night. She hoped the rings would be infused with this planetary energy. "Goodbye red moon," Olson had written in his poem "Moonset, Gloucester, December 1, 1957, 1:58 A.M.":

> In that color you set
> west of the Cut I should imagine
> forever Mother

Against this cosmic setting of visible planets and an oncoming snowstorm, I first heard the name Thelonious Monk. On the floor of the living room, Thorpe had stacked various LPs so that the first in the pile faced the guests as if announcing itself: *Solo Monk*. I crouched for a closer look. To pun on *solo*, the producers had commissioned an illustration of Monk in the cockpit of a yellow plane. A brown pilot's cap fits tight on his skull and a creamy white scarf flows across his neck before disappearing off the LP's edge. The scarf's color matches the big lenses in his goggles, strapped to the cap above his eyes, and Monk almost looks at you, though he doesn't look straight ahead, either.

"Who's that?" I asked Thorpe.

"That's Thelonious Monk."

"Who?"

"Thelonious Monk."

"Solo Monk?"

"Yeah, that's the name of the record. But *his* first name's Thelonious. Here—I'll put it on."

And in the company of painters and poets and musicians, and of my parents and other people's relatives, in the very apartment where Olson wrote sections II and III of his *Maximus Poems*, only a few feet from the bright wedding rings on the sill, Monk played "Dinah" and "Sweet and Lovely," "Monk's Point" and "I Should Care," "I Surrender, Dear" and "Ruby, My Dear." He played "These Foolish Things" and "I Hadn't Anyone Till You." He played "Ask Me Now."

Several times that evening, I insisted that Thorpe repeat this most magical of names, first unsure of the sound—*Thelonious*—and then unsure of the information—"Thelonious" as name. But I loved hearing it, and hearing it often. I'd laugh: "Say it again." And although it would be a few years before I listened to Monk again, and several more before I bought every available recording, I stared at Monk in the cockpit and listened with joy to his music. In the context of that wedding, even to the ears of a boy, Monk's music seemed absolutely perfect.

At the age of eight, I found the concept of planets burning energy into wedding rings to be downright silly, and yet don't we all have to decide individually where we draw the line between coincidence and spiritual connection? Do we ever fully negotiate fate and free will—and isn't there *something* planetary about the circularity of memory and experience?

In my twenties, I knew that the amnesial loss of my junior year had everything to do with repression—the limitations of my emotional system, how most people shut down during times of extreme stress—and for a while I thought I had fully come to terms with the psychology of lost memory. Wasn't it enough to *acknowledge* the loss? "Accept the fact that it's gone," I urged myself, "and move on." Ultimately, of course, that failed to clarify anything, and now, restructuring and reconsidering the dim rooms of experience, I am grateful for artifacts.

But I am skeptical of them, too. Though I think warmly of the imagined woman in the shop on Amsterdam Avenue, and almost expect to see that store when I walk the city streets, I know the making of that story generated personal knowledge far beyond the story itself. Even with the most famous writers, I think copious drafts of early work primarily benefit eager scholars.

Consider Thelonious Monk, for example, who left high school before finishing. As a teenager, he performed as an organist for the Union Baptist Church in New York City, and then he crossed the country with a woman known as part evangelist, part healer. (Monk said they played "Rock and roll or rhythm and blues," adding: "She preached and healed and we played. And then the congregation would sing.") It's not that I wouldn't love to have recordings from those formative years, but this took place a solid decade before his debut on Blue Note's *Genius of Modern Music*—classic sessions of "early Monk." He was thirty.

In 1927, at Worcester Classical High School, Charlie Olson was known less for his writing and more for his public speaking skills. How many early drafts of poetry did he leave in casual conversation, lost in the air to everyone but himself?

I don't know what I could or should have written in those 150 blank journal pages, but I know I transposed much of that text into saxophone notes, untaped melodies channeling through the window screens of the second floor of the Cape house. That summer, some friends said they could hear me practicing as they jogged down the street until they rounded the corner, heading, I suppose, for a cool shower, or a walk to collect beach glass, or to some unmarked location between their public and private homes.

# Black Pearls

"On first listening," the liner notes warn, "one might think that Coltrane's music was an example of raw Dionysian spirit untamed by the guiding hand of Apollo." On the cover: Coltrane photographed from below so that his whole torso rises magisterially, the saxophone angled from his mouth and plunging (so it seems) through the frame of the LP. His hair's shaved tight to the skull and his neck bulges from the white collar; with a spotlight from the front, colored theater floods from the side, and solid black background, his head looks as though it might explode.

*Black Pearls*. Or, more accurately, **BLACK PEARLS ■ JOHN COLTRANE**. I've never felt more intimidated by an album's packaging—unnaturally so. What had induced such anxiety? Why, for several years, did the image make me recoil?

The music itself was recorded on May 23, 1958, a year to the month before Coltrane's watershed recording, *Giant Steps*. Ranked against previous recording dates from '58 or '57—LPs such as *Coltrane, Lush Life, Traneing In, Soultrane*, or the magnificent *Blue*

*Train*—it seems pleasant, if not unremarkable. Listening to the music now, or any time in the past ten or fifteen years, I am overwhelmed by the lack of ferociousness that I used to associate with the album. There's plenty of energy, but it's not "raw Dionysian spirit."

The title cut is roughly thirteen minutes long, and it lopes along without any enormous rhythmic or tonal surprises. Coltrane's opening solo tumbles forward, but with nowhere near the melodic force that he'd embody in less than a year. Donald Byrd takes a couple of fine but fairly reserved trumpet choruses, and then Red Garland plays Red Garland. Paul Chambers follows with a solid but underrecorded bass solo; he trades fours with Art Taylor, who then offers a tight, restrained drum solo. And then the band replays the bouncy melody.

The second and last tune on side A, the standard "Lover Come Back to Me," has no more edge, harmonically, but the tempo's breathtaking—so much so that Taylor seems to struggle to maintain the heat. "Sweet Sapphire Blues," an eighteen-minute cut that comprises all of side B, opens with about six minutes of Garland before Coltrane enters. Trane solos for four minutes, but his statement is not a radical departure from the choruses on the other two tunes. *Black Pearls* is a transitional recording, one that allowed him to create the astonishing sessions for Atlantic from 1959 to 1961. Why, then, did I fear the LP?

I knew it had nothing to do with warnings in the liner notes. (Even as a teenager, I never blindly accepted criticism.) Nor could the cover—which now just looks like a fine, somewhat overdramatized portrait of a heroic figure in my life—have possibly generated such an extreme response. Could I place the LP in my memory the way we reshelve records or CDs and locate that history? I kept playing the recording, hoping that music, as it so often does, would recover lost impressions. Then I stared at the album until my eyes unfocused the way Coltrane's saxophone does on the cover, refracted light off the keys blurring to circles, the bell shadowed into the background—image and mind blurring enough to reach the transitive point between consciousness and unconsciousness—until I could see an old woman in a chair placed close to my mother's bedside, and she gave me the answer.

This woman's name was Edna, and she was one of a great many visitors that year. Most of the people who came to our house were close friends, mainly artists whom I knew quite well. Some did not visit often and, when they did, didn't stay long; others, in a selfishness that often accompanies such visitations, prolonged their visits until they had thoroughly exhausted my mother. I'm not sure whether anyone can master the art of spending time with a terminally ill friend, but some did much better than others.

And then there were the people whom I knew at best by name and who seemed like minor characters in a foreign film. Some had known me as a baby, and I had all the conversations that teenagers never want to have. Wrinkled hands patted my cheek. Near-strangers wept. The impulse, of course, was to say, "Yes. I was small; now I'm big. This is awful. Get away." (As a child, my mother's brother had apparently peered up at his great aunts, all dressed in black and leaning over his small bed, and had shouted in Swedish, "You're all a bunch of witch crows!" How I envied his smart mouth.) When close friends came, I felt comforted and grateful, but when our home filled with unrecognizable guests, it seemed as though we had the Saddest Show on Earth, and almost everybody had a ticket.

Among that crowd was Edna, who did everything she could to ease our sorrow, and whose actions bewildered me. I also felt intimidated by her. She had an English accent and she carried herself not with the prissiness often associated with the upper-class English but nevertheless with a British formality. She seemed not at all judgmental, and yet she emanated a sense of learnedness that made me cower.

She visited our house several times, and at least twice she stopped by on the weekends, when I was not in school. She was thin and energetic, and she wanted to talk with me, and during our poor exchanges I kept asking myself, "Who are you, and why are you making me speak?" I don't, in fact, remember a single sentence. But she must have spoken to my father and asked about my interests, and he must have told her that I loved jazz. I know this because she had gifts for me when we met on those weekends, and they were jazz LPs, both by John Coltrane: *Ascension* and *Black Pearls*.

What Edna knew about jazz could probably have formed half a

haiku, but, to be fair, I didn't know very much about jazz, either. I was sixteen, I had been listening to the music only for about three years, and my self-education had not been systematic or academic. It began in the living room, before I started sleeping there, when the thought of cancer seemed far more abstract than music. I'd been listening to pop—not Top 40, but the kind of I'm-Down-and-Out country-rock schlock you'd hear from most locally famous guitarists in upstate New York. I thought they were hip.

One afternoon, I discovered a cut that I particularly enjoyed and insisted that it be played for my father and Thorpe. They didn't squash my enthusiasm, exactly, but I could tell they found the music utterly insipid. My father stood up and said, "Let me put on some records so you'll know there was music before the Beatles," and he spun *Kid Ory's Creole Jazz Band 1954* on the Good Time Jazz label. Then he played the better stuff—Coleman Hawkins. You'd think my adolescent chutzpah would have told him to shove it. You know: "Thanks, Dad, for taking me down your memory lane, but that shit's ancient." Instead, my whole body filled with one enormous response: *This is better than what I know. This is astonishing.*

Naturally, my teenage pride didn't give in to words, and I didn't fully acknowledge how badly I'd been beaten in this skirmish of aesthetics, but Thorpe spotted my enthusiasm and began to pass along more jazz records. Then my father unearthed volumes of jazz LPs that he had acquired over the years. Most were used, some were discards from the street (I learned how to repair minor scratches with the graphite from pencils), and some were in mint condition.

Of the swing players, Hawkins became my tenor player of choice. I loved the sweetness of Johnny Hodges and the breathiness of Ben Webster, but Hawkins had such muscularity to his phrasing and, besides, he was one of the first voices I'd heard. (Do we ever love any music more?) I found bebop irresistible and hummed bop tunes throughout the day. And I listened to a great deal of hard bop, seeking out the Blue Note logos on my father's old records. Even today, when little Pee Wee Marquette announces, "Welcome to Birdland, ladies and gentleman," my mind spirals to New York: twenty years to reach my father's brownstone, and then twenty-six more, until it's 1954, nine years before my birth, but I'm in the room—actually in the club, right near the stand—eye level with Art Blakey and Clifford Brown and Lou Donaldson and Curley Russell and Horace Silver, and they're about to change my life forever with "Split Kick" and "Once in a While."

But Coltrane—what music of his did I know? For certain, I had listened to his solos on *Monk's Music*. (I remember hearing Thelonious Monk call out, "*Coltrane*, Coltrane," though I didn't know the history behind that cue.) And I know we had a copy of Miles Davis's *'Round Midnight*, although, for whatever reason, my ears focused on Miles, not Trane. I definitely knew him by name, but I barely touched on his work as a sideman, and I can't remember a single John Coltrane album in the house—a statement that seems impossible but appears to be true.

Nor do I recall what I said to Edna when she handed me Coltrane's *Ascension*, but I remember being absolutely unprepared for the music. It was fifteen years old—recorded during the summer of 1965—and I want to say it jarred me with the same intensity that it had others after its initial release. Because I had heard nothing that approximated this sound. Because the cover (Coltrane meditative on a music stool, the background completely white except for his name and the multicolored letters of the title rising to the top right) seems Buddha-like in its passivity. Because I dropped the needle onto the turntable before reading, if I ever read them at all, A. B. Spellman's liner notes:

> To begin at the beginning, a caveat for the casual listener. Be advised that this record cannot be loved or understood in one sitting, and that there can be no appreciation at all in two minutes listening to an arbitrary excerpt in a record store. In fact, there is no casual approach to be taken to this record. It is truly modern; it is as advanced as the most advanced contemporary jazz is and, the communications scene being as retarded as it is, the kind of event which *Ascension* is will be unfamiliar to anyone who has not made it a serious avocation to search out and understand the new jazz.

Very rarely will you find liner notes so accurate and instructive. At that time in my life, I was very much a "casual listener"; no art meant more to me—not painting, not poetry, not anything—but I didn't *know* jazz, and certainly not "the new jazz."

I had headphones on. Downstairs, it was time for morphine injections, and that meant absolute quiet. I heard the LP-hiss that we've lost with CDs, and then *Ascension* unfurled: those famous opening statements by Coltrane and Pharoah Sanders and Archie Shepp (tenor saxophones) *and* Marion Brown and John Tchicai (altos) *and* Freddie Hubbard and Dewey Johnson (trumpets)—all of them, their musical lines over and beneath each other, horns riding the grounding basses of Art Davis and Jimmy Garrison, McCoy Tyner coloring the background as though piano chords could drop with the piano itself from above the stage. And Elvin Jones establishing an utterly open rhythm—brief drum rolls and the *dish, Dish,,, DISH* of cymbals—until the whole world seems to collapse into sound. All this in the first two minutes of a performance that lasts almost forty.

*Ascension* exhausts the listener with a nearly unrivaled intensity. Some have called it a post-nuclear statement. Others think of it as apocalyptic. I remember feeling as though I had experienced a car crash involving several vehicles, where some people had been killed and most others severed from their limbs—screams and blood, with more and more oncoming cars. Windshields exploding. Tires gripping heated asphalt. Brakes. And, again, the human response to it all. "We did two takes," said Marion Brown, "and they both had that kind of thing in them that makes people scream. The people who were in the studio *were* screaming. I don't know how the engineers kept the screams out of the record."

There is no way in heaven or hell that Edna had heard this music.

And yet, in reflection, it's quite easy to imagine her making the purchase. Edna walks into Sam Goody's or Disc-O-Mat and tells an employee that she wants to buy a *jazz* album. "He's a teenager and he plays the saxophone." She doesn't tell him what's going on at the home, and he doesn't give her a title, just a name: Coltrane. She walks to the bins and, though the jazz selection in general has been badly depleted since the 1970s, she finds too many choices under the artist's name. Maybe she's in a hurry; maybe the man has walked away. But she's on her own now, and she guides her selection by alphabetical listing: A, then B; *Ascension, Black Pearls.* "I'll give him one today," she thinks, "the other at my next visit." She hopes it will be a small comfort.

Here's a near-parallel scenario. Someone who doesn't know serious fiction tries to buy an important work for a kid who wants to be a writer. The good-hearted, well-meaning purchaser walks into a large bookstore and asks for the name of a literary giant. "James Joyce." But the person doesn't buy *Dubliners* or *Portrait* or even *Ulysses*. Instead, by happenstance, or perhaps under the assumption that an author's last work is probably the most satisfying, she brings the teenager, who up until that point has mainly encountered the *Norton Anthology of Short Fiction*, Joyce's *Finnegans Wake*.

That analogy, however, seems inadequate in terms of threat. A kid reading *Finnegans Wake* could easily dismiss it: "This is gobbledygook. I don't care what my teacher says." But sound has the emotional edge on literature in terms of immediate impact. Unlike words on the page—read well or poorly, at the reader's pace—music comes *to* us. Information arrives quickly, and sometimes unforgettably so.

Edna had meant well and was genuinely kind, but I resented everything about her. For one, I literally could not comprehend why someone would give a gift—any gift—to a person she didn't know. Mainly, though, I resented her for entangling my passion for jazz with such emotional complexity, such confusion. I thought to myself as she handed me the album, "She must know Coltrane—I guess I know next to nothing about the music," and I was half right. And then, later, as my mother began to slip into a morphine dream and as the headphones began to push the blood from my ears, I thought, "This is the most frightening music ever created." I heard the sounds not as an ascension towards serenity but as a Dantean descent straight to the center of my own collapsing world.

Which is why I don't think I ever broke the cellophane on *Black Pearls*. I certainly have no memory of it, except for the cover image. She probably asked if I enjoyed the other album, and I'm sure I said, "Yes." But I suspect I rejected *Black Pearls* the way children often refuse to retry a food they've disliked in the past, nor did I replay *Ascension* for many months.

Once my mother became completely bedridden, Edna didn't

return. I kept the Coltrane albums in my collection and flipped by them, always turning instead to Miles Davis, Duke Ellington, Art Farmer, Stan Getz, Coleman Hawkins—music that preceded the free jazz of the late 1960s—and though I probably thought of her when I saw Coltrane's image, I can't say I noticed her absence. But I'm aware of it now, too late to thank her for the spirit of her gift and, beyond that, for the gift itself. Because when I listen to *Ascension*—as I did this afternoon in the study of my new home, where sunlight almost whitens the oak floor—I wonder whether I didn't encounter this music at exactly the right time, whether the experience of loss and love, and of strangers offering what they can in the spirit of sympathy, didn't allow an entrance into the wildly complicated music of Coltrane's final years.

Some gifts, I guess, we have to grow into; others are more immediately satisfying. While I could make no sense of Edna's presents, I understood absolutely why my mother wanted her closest friends to own some of her work. Three days before she died, my father took a series of her paintings—acrylic on paper, roughly two by three feet—and spread them across the floor. Then friends selected the painting they wanted most. Nothing had been signed, and my mother, elevated by a bed we'd rented from the hospital, labored to write her name on the back of each image. In one case, she didn't like the painting—didn't want anyone to choose it—and printed her name in a way that made it seem like a forgery.

Most people had a noticeably difficult time selecting a piece, mainly because of the magnitude of the whole experience, but also because of the works' quality. These were not sketches or juvenilia; these were expansive statements made by an artist in her prime. Friends would say things like, "It's too much," or, "How am I to choose?" This was the gift of a legacy. Placed on a wall, in an individual's home, each would make its own statement and carry with it unique associative memories. But spread out across the floor, one vibrant gesture beside another, playing off one another, the paintings seemed to transfer color across the carpet, some sinking beneath the surface, others rising. They simply overwhelmed our eyes.

A year later, as a high school senior, I took a class in music theory from Paul Betjeman, a brilliant and eccentric teacher who seemed to share none of the tame conservatism of his father, one of England's former poet laureates. Betjeman's room had a low ceiling and a large table that consumed most of the floor space. Against every wall, he had set up various pieces of equipment (keyboards, tape players, speakers, equalizers, amplifiers, turntables), and, as a result, students had barely enough room to pull out their chairs.

There weren't many students in his classes. For one, my peers tended to dismiss the arts in favor of business or science courses. For another, Betjeman often came across as a madman—exploding with strings of profanity when, for example, he'd misplaced a pitch pipe (which he did often)—and this, coupled with his naturally distracted demeanor, made them fear him. Signing up for one of his courses, a student could be assured of only one thing: the class would be small.

I didn't particularly enjoy music theory (in my high school yearbook, Betjeman wrote simply, "Develop a harmonic approach to improvisation"), but I loved those classes, and I loved every outrageous moment. Our musical tastes did not overlap exactly—he seemed most passionate about electronic music, which left me cold—but he really knew jazz and had once been a serious baritone saxophonist, traveling with jazz bands in Europe while his family back in England shook their heads dismissively. One afternoon, I mentioned my great excitement at hearing for the first time Gerry Mulligan's 1957 recording *What Is There To Say?* Betjeman laughed at me. I said, "Don't you like it?"

"Yes," he replied, softening to a more sympathetic tone. "Of course. It's just that you're listening to the same things I listened to when I was about your age."

I never wanted to *be* Paul Betjeman, but I knew he had an understanding of jazz that far exceeded my experience and knowledge, either as a player or a listener. And I wanted him to like me, to find me worth his time, but it was difficult to engage him in lengthy conversations, or even short ones. With some embarrassment now, I remember walking to our local bookstore, long since defunct, and buying a collection by his father, John Betjeman, whose work I didn't know. (I didn't know what a poet laureate was, either.) I spent a few days with the book, and while it didn't fully interest me, I found some images that I liked and could appreciate his facility with form.

"I bought a book by your father," I said to him after class.

"Oh," he replied, which was exactly the right response, though somehow I had expected a pat-on-the-head gesture and some gateway into a conversation.

"I like some of the poems," I said.

"He's very English." Betjeman scattered papers across the wide table but did not look remotely in my direction.

"I like some of the landscapes," I said after another awkward pause.

"Yes, well, he's very English."

Even my thick head registered that this would be the end of our discussion.

My efforts to make him talk often fell flat. Sometimes, though, I'd mention a recording that he particularly loved—Sonny Rollins's version of "You Don't Know What Love Is," for example, from *Saxophone Colossus*—and he would become, if not completely engaged, at least passionately responsive. Sometimes I would ask him to recommend recordings, and sometimes—not often, but sometimes—he'd oblige. "Oliver Nelson's *Screamin' the Blues*," he once answered. "Nelson plays the way he arranges, but listen to the other soloists."

And then one day, perhaps because I never mentioned Coltrane, Betjeman asked if I had listened much to his work. Headphones: *Ascension*. I felt overwhelmed with memory, knew I didn't have much time for an answer, and replied foolishly:

"I don't like his tone."

Betjeman looked noticeably disappointed, but he responded quite directly to my statement.

"Oh, but he spent a long time creating that tone. He really wanted that sound." Then he asked, "Do you know *Giant Steps*?"

I didn't. Admitting that now seems like the humblest of statements—like not knowing Mozart or Rembrandt or water—but I was too naïve to know naïveté. Betjeman pinched the edge of the record from its sleeve and slipped it onto the player. He turned the volume up (he always turned the volume up, no matter what the setting had been), and suddenly that tiny room ignited with the fire of "Mr. P.C." Like my previous experience with Coltrane, I had nothing to prepare me for this sound—not even Coltrane, for I had not yet heard *Black Pearls* and didn't know where Trane had been before *Ascension*. I had never heard such command and strength, such unrelenting phrases. And it was thrilling—genuinely thrilling—every bit as much as my first encounter with jazz. The spiraling phrases of John Coltrane transformed that tiny room into an amphitheater open to the sky.

The cut concluded, he picked up the needle, and I said, "Oh my God."

I went straight from school to the record store and bought my own copy. For a long time, I didn't play anything else.

# Mormor

My grandmother lived an impulsive, if not irresponsible, life, and my mother never fully came to terms with her upbringing. Often, my grandmother became enraged over an event unknown to her family, or at a child's poor behavior, and she would snatch her coat from the rack, thrust the door open, and, before leaving, yell, "I'm never coming back." My mother remembered many afternoons sitting by the window, for hours sometimes, wondering whether her near-silent father had become her only parent.

But there were wonderful stories, too, and, as a child, those were the ones I knew. One morning in her youth, for example, she saw that bottles of milk had been delivered and, though she wasn't wearing any clothes, leapt outside to grasp the crate's handle. (It was very early and she had planned a quick leap.) But the front door closed and locked behind her, and she began to crawl along the hedges towards her friend's home. The neighbors across the street, however, saw the dappled outline of a crouching, naked figure behind the shrubs, assumed it was a pervert, and telephoned the police, who arrived swiftly. "She grabbed for the milk," my father later said, "and they nabbed the cow."

Another time, her best friend asked for advice about cleaning fur because her husband had a fabulously expensive hat that had been stored during the summer and now seemed a bit musty. My grandmother had heard that plaster worked well—which is true, if you dust the fur and then remove the plaster, but not true, as she learned, if you add water as directed.

Her visits were never without incident. Once, the day she arrived, she complained of back pains and only that evening realized she hadn't removed the coat hanger from her dress. Better still was the time my mother picked her up at JFK. They chatted by the luggage conveyor belt, waiting for the bags to emerge. My grandmother was about seventy then, and, always stylish, she wore a scarlet beret. When she saw her suitcase emerge on the belt, she didn't wait for my mother and, in a gesture that must have approximated her reach for the milk crate, lunged at the handle. But the suitcase was heavy—very heavy—and slipped from her fingers. She saw the bag turning towards the rubber stripping that covers the conveyor belt's opening, and part of her must have thought this was her only chance to retrieve her belongings, because she then hopped on the belt itself and gripped the handle with both hands. By the time she balanced herself, however, the suitcase was inches from the exit, and, instead of letting go, she ducked and disappeared.

A couple of minutes later, my mother saw the bag reappear through the rubber stripping, and then the red beret, and then her mother—my *mormor* (literally, in Swedish, "mother's mother")—who swung the suitcase over the side and said, "*Ja,* now we can go."

I have often tried to imagine the airport workers hustling behind the wall, lurching and heaving, sweating through the job they probably never wanted, and suddenly seeing a smartly dressed old woman riding the conveyor belt as if it were a carousel. But as a kid, it was more than enough to recall the crowd at the baggage claim, and every time my mother told that story, I laughed until I could hardly breathe.

To me, she was the funniest woman in history. To my father, she was an idiot. (He once claimed that she had "wedges of brain missing.") They never got along. She distrusted him in part because of the age difference between my parents—he was seventeen years older than my mother, and only ten years younger than my grandmother—and she must have worried, too, about the financial challenges that two artists would confront. My father was not blind to this, so, shortly after proposing, he sent my grandmother a six-page letter, explaining how much he loved her daughter, declaring his sense of responsibility, and so on. As far as we know, she never read the letter. Instead, she took it to a handwriting analyst, who told her he was a genius, so she approved of the marriage. But despite that glowing appraisal, Dad resented her judging the letter—perhaps the longest of his life—by style rather than content.

He also knew of my mother's oppressive childhood, and I don't think he ever understood why she forgave her mother for the explosive moods and the threats of abandonment. No, he never understood that. But his love for his wife overcame his hatred for his mother-in-law, and when my mother's diagnosis became clear, he sent an airplane ticket to my grandmother. She stayed with us for several months, arriving after the diagnosis had been labeled terminal, and leaving three days after my mother died.

At least once each afternoon, my grandmother walked vigorously through Riverside Park. I rarely joined her. For one, she walked too quickly, not outpacing me, but never slowing down to acknowledge *anything*, river to monument. Her heels clicked across the concrete promenade with an intensity and rhythm that approximated a ball on a never-ending roulette wheel. She'd walk not in the most beautiful areas but in the widest spaces. She'd walk in snow and rain, against high winds that pulled tears from her eyes. She walked and walked, punishing the paths.

At home, I remember being grateful to her for helping us with meals, and sometimes I'd help her in the kitchen. (After she returned to Sweden, I became the cook.) For all her wildness and ultimate lack of interest in domesticity, she could create wonderful dinners and genuinely astonishing desserts. On one occasion—Valentine's Day, perhaps—she baked and decorated a cake with such professionalism that no one wanted to eat it. She'd carved and placed a sugary red rose atop green bayberry-like leaves. How had this woman, who most often acted with the subtlety of a spinning drill bit, slowed herself long enough to transform colored sugar into a flower so lifelike it could fool a honeybee?

When I practiced my saxophones, she most often left me alone. But when I took out my clarinet to play classical music, she sometimes walked upstairs, sat in a chair, and listened. Once, she wept throughout the practice. I kept playing, movement to movement, forcing myself not to stop; she always made me feel as though her grief was *her* grief. Nor did I hear her, but from across the room, peering above the sheet music, I watched tears streak her face. She'd wipe her eyes, turn the page of a magazine she may or may not have been reading, then wipe her eyes again.

I had a sense that she loved me, and that she dearly loved her dying daughter, but neither of us shared emotions very well. Rarely did she offer an affectionate gesture, and that was okay with me, too. Besides, if our relationship verged on neutrality, it nevertheless felt worlds closer than the iciness she cultivated with my father. I hated being around them at the same time, even though she guarded her emotions and words with a Scandinavian stolidity, and he guarded his with the pride of a Russian immigrant.

That resolve of unspoken anger lasted until the final two weeks of my mother's life. Everyone had stopped trying to save her, except for my father. He had heard of experimental cancer drugs from Hungary and needed a urine sample. By then, my mother had wasted to near nothingness, her body so dehydrated that it took two or three days for him to get that sample. (He kept insisting—"Try. Just try. Don't think about it. No rush."—but I could see his anxiety swell with each hour, each day.) Finally, he got what he needed. The amount barely discolored the bottom of the glass, but it was enough. He ran to the door, then realized that the post office had long been closed, and placed the glass beneath the bathroom sink. He'd mail it in the morning.

What would have been the ideal outcome? What had he hoped

for? That the US mail would be better than it was, and that the Hungarian mail would be better than that (already an impossibility)? That the labs in Hungary would analyze the sample immediately and, with equal speed, send along the appropriate wonder drug? That this medicine would treat last-stage cancer with unheard-of thoroughness, and that, soon, my mother would rise to begin the second half of her life? Could he have hoped for this?

The post office opened at 8:30. I suspect my father rose that morning at 5:00 or 6:00. I heard my grandmother walk downstairs at 6:30 and begin to clean the kitchen. My mother slept, having been dreadfully conscious for most of the night. (I knew she didn't have enough morphine, could hear her at various hours from midnight to dawn.) My alarm went off at 7:00 and I prepared for school. I must have been downstairs by 7:30 . . .

I'm sitting at the kitchen table. I have already given my grandmother a "good morning" hug and poured some juice. She's at the sink. Then the screaming begins:

*Where's the glass?*

My father runs into the kitchen.

*Where the hell is the glass—the one beneath the bathroom sink? Where the hell did it go?*

Then he spots it in the dish drainer, lunges for the glass as if he were tightening his fingers on a throat, and realizes instantly it's been washed clean.

*Oh my God! Oh . . . my God!*

He's crying now. My grandmother cries, too—still not comprehending why a filthy glass could be important—and heads for the stairs, but not before he yells at her rising heels:

*Why did you DO this? You haven't done ANYTHING since . . . Oh my God! Why did you DO this?*

And they're howling, and now I can hear my mother weeping from behind the partially closed doors.

And I am standing now. For several minutes, I can't move. My father has disappeared to my mother's room. I can still hear my grandmother. My bag of books and saxophone rest by the door. Soon, I think to myself, I will sit in the backseat, the daily car pool—Jane and a history teacher—and they will ask me how things are, and I will say, "Not so good," and they'll say, "I'm sorry." And then, miles away: another day of school . . .

Before I left the house that morning, I poured the rest of my juice down the sink. I couldn't swallow, and I wouldn't cry. I thought if I broke down, there would be nothing left. Nothing. I put a little bit of soap on a new, blue sponge, turned it slowly along the inside of the glass, and thought, "You have to be strong. Nothing else will save you." I rinsed off the soap and dried my hands—hypnotic motions my grandmother must have shared: *I can make this glass clean*—and then I crossed the straps of my book bag and saxophone case. "If you're not strong, your world will fall apart." It was probably the most damaging decision I've ever made.

My mother died about ten days later, and three days after that the house was utterly transformed. My grandmother left for Sweden, and I didn't see her for six years. Men in gray overalls retrieved the rented hospital bed. My father boxed the bottles of morphine and the syringes and bandages and tubes. (Five years later, I found that box, next to one filled with sympathy cards.) We removed everything related to her cancer, and I remember how, when we opened windows and doors, the April air swept through the house with a baptismal purity. I stood in the middle of the brownstone, with the spring air and the brighter light, and, with the same irrational faith that my father placed in the medicine from Hungary, thought, "I can live again. This is the start of a new life. Everything that's happened is in the past, gone." At that moment, I fully believed I could package grief and store it in the heart's fifth chamber.

My father never communicated with my grandmother again, and if her name was raised in conversation, he'd squash the subject instantly, referring to her with a demeaning nickname, usually fresh, always acerbic. For a few years, I felt as though I couldn't mention her even in passing, and most of the time that restriction posed no difficulty, since I housed my own ill feelings about her visit and rarely explored that "lost year" in conversations. Nor did I communicate frequently with my relatives in Sweden. I left for college in 1981, graduated in 1985, then took a year off before accepting a fellowship in English at Indiana University; after several months as a substitute teacher in Rochester's public high schools, I looked forward to the comforting, known perimeters of academe.

By 1986, however, I also wanted very much to revisit my mother's homeland. It had been eleven years since my last trip to Sweden, and I had never made a significant journey by myself. I saved throughout the year, received a Eurail Pass as a birthday present, and planned a three-month trip through Europe, starting with two weeks in Stockholm. My father, elated about my grad school plans, bought me a professional hiker's backpack, which I loaded with a minimal amount of clothing, a blank notebook, and Yeats's *Selected Poems*. (Carrying my alto saxophone as well, I must have looked a little like a one-man band.) His delight in my academic goals temporarily eclipsed his hatred of my grandmother. I remember him saying, "Send her my loathe," but nothing more than that.

My grandmother and Uncle Jan (the elder of two uncles, and the only one with a family) waited for me in the airport and greeted me with genuine warmth, though my arrival undoubtedly brought great pain as well. As we walked through the airport, my grandmother mainly spoke in brief, one-syllable interjections—"*Ja*," "Mmm," or a quick inhale—but she didn't seem to be responding to any observation or statement. Her interjections burst as randomly as sparks from a fallen power line.

For Uncle Jan, the associations were no less painful, but he could partially disconnect himself, having never seen my mother during her final year. He had wanted to come to America, to be with his only sister, his closest relative, but simply couldn't bear the grief. Instead, he sent his beautiful wife, Kristina, who stayed with us for a matter of days. Oh, how I wanted her to stay longer. But she had to return for a reason I knew and understood—her own mother had cancer, and the cancer got much worse shortly after her arrival—and for a bizarre reality that she kept secret. (I learned of this years later.) When she stepped off the plane in America, jet fumes induced extreme nausea, and, like many women who know their bodies with psychic accuracy, she correctly diagnosed her condition: "Oh my God," she said to herself. "I'm pregnant." She was in her late forties and had three grown children. So she returned to Sweden to abort the fetus and bury her mother.

Stockholm can be damp and dark—most winter visitors understand quickly why the Swedes drink hard—and spring that year had been nonexistent. My grandmother urged me to bring warm clothing. I paid little attention to her warning, however, and got very lucky. When the three of us stepped outside the airport, the evergreens shimmered in bright sunlight, and for the two weeks of my stay, I don't recall one rainy day. ("The best two weeks of Sweden for the past two years," my uncle later told me.) Jan drove us to my grandmother's apartment, which had a guest room, and we saw each other several times during my stay, including a dinner at his home with Kristina, all three of their children, her sister and brother-in-law, and my other uncle, Jörgen, the funniest man in the family. Jörgen could bust up a room just by wiggling his ears, but most of that evening he spent elsewhere: in the woods, in other rooms—I'm just not sure.

No one, it seemed, could disassociate my presence from their profound, unspoken sadness. They very much wanted me to visit, and yet they had difficulty looking at my face. They decorated their houses and apartments with my mother's paintings and weavings, but they never said a word about her life or death. No conversation, in fact, flowed easily, although that had something to do with language itself: I'd never been taught any Swedish, and, with the standard arrogance of an American traveler, I relied on everyone else to speak English. They wanted me to be there, but each time I left a relative's home, I imagined him or her exhaling deeply. Never before or since have I been the epicenter of such emotional upheaval.

So out of courtesy, and my own desire, I spent most of each day by myself, walking the streets and playing my saxophone for strangers. Most often, I'd play at the archway that separates modern Stockholm from Gamla Stan, the Old Town. It is a stunning location, right on the water where large ships from Finland cruise into the harbor, and, again, the weather blessed us universally, sending the Swedes into tangible euphoria. I played old standards; they tossed money like wealthy farmers sowing seeds. I made about twenty bucks an hour, and when I left Sweden I had more money than when I arrived.

I also ate lavishly. After an hour or two by the harbor, I'd bag my collection of Swedish kroner, pack up the alto, and meander through Gamla Stan until I came across a hidden, interesting-looking restaurant. I'd order a beer or chilled Akvavit, take out my notepad, and write down images of the day while awaiting salmon in dill sauce, or scalloped potatoes with salted bacon and thick cream, or tender meatballs with lingonberries. Several times, I saved a coaster or printed napkin and, at the end of the day, showed the name to my grandmother. "Oh yes," she said, almost each time. "That was one of Anita's favorite restaurants."

Was she projecting another life onto mine, imagining a preferred truth? Was this purely coincidental, or could it be true that my mother's spirit took me by the hand through the snaking back streets of Stockholm, introducing me to the places and foods she loved in her youth?

And did my grandmother even acknowledge the coincidental nature of this experience? I don't know. She spoke English quite well, but sparingly. Everything else in her life seemed absolutely controlled. Each morning, perfectly displayed after I showered and dressed: tight corners on the breakfast tablecloth, bright cutlery, orange juice and coffee, butter and cheese, boiled eggs, crusty Wasa bread, jams and local spreads. I don't know how she spent the rest of her day.

The morning I left, she had great difficulty composing herself. She spoke in fragments about being a poor mother—no, a terrible mother. She wiped tears with gestures that edged on fury. She talked of guilt without redemption, of never being forgiven. Never. And I tried to console her, but she did not want to hear from me. She simply wanted me to know that she understood where she had failed and that she'd never settled this with her daughter, and never could. Then she kissed me, hard, on the cheek, said, "Now you must go," and half-pushed me out the door.

I thought about that morning for the rest of the day as I walked from her apartment to the underground train station, and then to the main terminal from which I spent many hours riding to Denmark.

For the first time, I pitied my grandmother, and for years afterwards, in letters and on subsequent visits, I tried to alleviate her guilt, but who can speak for the dead?

And can the dead speak to us? The night before I left Sweden, while I restuffed my belongings into my backpack, I sensed with remarkable clarity my mother's soundless voice. I said to myself, "You're being ridiculous," and then I almost—or do I even need to say *almost?*—felt a tap on my shoulder. I knew my mother wanted to talk with me, to speak to me. This had never happened before, and I found myself saying, out loud, "I can't talk right now. I have to pack. I have to get ready for my trip tomorrow." At that moment, the overhead light in the room flickered, then blinked out, and before I said, "Okay, Mom, you win," before she really did speak to me to make sure that I would open myself fully to the experience of travel, I found myself sitting in absolute blackness, and laughing.

# Before

Sympathy cards arrived by the basketful, and each day after school I'd spot the new ones sorted and placed in a bright yellow bowl on the kitchen table. From there, my father brought them to his writing desk because, for whatever complex reasons, he felt determined to answer every note, from passionate letters to Hallmark cards. I didn't understand his sense of obligation and encouraged him to leave them alone. "No one's expecting a reply," I'd say. "Look—some have even written 'Please don't feel the need to write back.'" I don't think he ever heard me. I'd begin my homework, and he would work on his correspondence. I never saw what he wrote and don't know whether he talked about my mother's death, or her life, or simply expressed his gratitude for their concern, but I remember being aware, somehow, of his writing coming to a slow close, and I wasn't at all surprised when I overheard him tell a student, "I've stopped responding to the sympathy cards. I tried for a while, but I just can't do it anymore."

Of the letters I received, the one I remember most vividly came from two boys I knew on Cape Cod. They had written the card together, and one mentioned a visit he had made to our house in New York—how he felt "homesick" after leaving. He said that he had learned so much from my mother and that she "was so pretty and full of enthusiasm." Then he added: "She *still* is, because that is the way we will always remember her. Please forget the way you saw her the past few months and remember her the way she was before, all your life."

All my life. The way she was before. His words haunted me for the rest of that day, and all week, and they returned at unexpected times for years to come. His words sounded so pure and true, but I was psychologically unable to act on them. With the best of intentions, he had cast a benevolent curse. "Remember her the way she was before."

Each time I tried to imagine her youthful face, my mind superimposed a skeletal death mask from her final weeks. I could replay afternoons when we walked through the cedar swamp on Cape Cod or held hands through the heavily trafficked streets of downtown Manhattan, but in a moment I would be in the hallway again, holding her arm, moving at the excruciatingly slow pace of an anxiety dream, desperately guiding her to the bathroom. And then, in a shelling of nightmare, I'd revisit the artifacts of cancer: the stacks of cardboard bowls placed at her bedside; the paint box now filled with morphine bottles and syringes; her stomach distended; her bones curving; the furniture, even more dimly lit in memory, now also distended and curving. I could not *get* to "the way she was before." I tried during the meditative hours of night, and the dramatic sunlight of day, but I just could not get there.

I don't know how long this lasted, nor am I sure whether I'll ever recover unblemished childhood memories, though, in the most general terms, I recall only a lovely, sentimental joyousness when I think of childhood, and it's rare that a particular memory does not include my mother. I spent many summer hours, for example, exploring the beach and building supernatural worlds out of sand, and although I almost always worked by myself, I knew she sat only a few yards away, sketch pad on her lap as she drew her own imagined worlds with a fine black line or an assortment of bold, felt-tipped pens. At the beach, and in most other settings, she established a wonderful parental balance that I could not have consciously appreciated as a boy; in a literal and metaphoric sense, she encouraged me to swim by myself, but her cautious eyes made certain I didn't swim too far from shore.

Given my known passions for painting and music, she also knew how fortunate I was to have parents who loved the arts. Much like my father's family, her conservative parents and relatives had no artistic sensibilities—or at least none that they nurtured—and made little effort to encourage her creative drives. During her youth, she never felt respected. "Nobody ever asked if you had an opinion about anything," she told a teacher of mine in January 1979, when she and my father were interviewed for a project concerning generations of parents and children. "It took many years to find out what you wanted to do. My mother was not fulfilled in having three kids . . . I think you have to feel really good to be a good parent."

In that same taped conversation, the interviewer asks what my parents would like me to be and if they had tried to steer me towards the arts. In response, they explain how they've guided, but not molded, my own interests. "I truly hope to be around long enough to see him get on his own feet and take his place," my father says, adding, "That's about it." But my mother sounds more forceful and directed in her wishes: "I'd like him to be an artist. I think that's the best life—something you can grow into for the rest of your life. But only if he wants. If he wants to be a musician—or whatever. I don't care . . . if it's music, or writing, for that matter. A poet. Anything that holds the doors open all your life."

Listening to her speak—and I didn't hear this taped exchange until twenty years later—I am caught between two internal dialogues. On the one hand, her words do not surprise me, not even the fleeting reference to poetry, a possibility she never mentioned to me directly; on the other, I'm reminded yet again of our relationship's natural limitations, how I never had the opportunity to speak to her as an adult. Perhaps one of the reasons I had so much trouble remembering her "as she was before" has to do with age: I kept searching for profound, mature conversations, but I kept revisiting, at best, the ambiguity of adolescence.

What would we have discussed? How to choose, and where to begin? I think I would have asked more about her emergence as an artist and about the complex relationship that she sustained with her mother. I would have asked how she managed to balance so remarkably her responsibilities as an artist and a parent. (Most of the world's most celebrated artists have been dreadful parents.) I would like to hear again the stories she *did* tell me, and to hear them with new ears.

Many nights during my childhood, as a way of postponing sleep but also out of genuine interest, I asked to hear stories of my mother's life when she was a young girl. Given the dozens of nights and the many incidents recounted at my request, I would have to say I remember the rhythm of her voice more than specific details. But I do recall several stories that involved narrow escapes. In one, the neighborhood jerk dropped a large stone on her head and almost split her skull. In another, her sleeve caught fire from a candle, and though she badly burned her arm, she would not tell her mother because she feared being punished. Similarly, one summer when the family vacationed on an island in southern Sweden, she pulled a rented canoe onto shore and ripped a massive hole in its center. She knew that the vacation itself had stretched the family's finances and that this accident might be disastrous. But that episode, like most of them, had a good ending: in an absolutely atypical gesture, my grandmother had purchased renters' insurance, and the family didn't have to shell out a single öre.

I had favorites, and some I asked repeatedly to hear, especially this one: Shortly after the Second World War, my mother's family had again located a pleasant country house to rent for a summer vacation. Early one morning, my grandmother, roughly forty at the time, emerged from their secluded cabin to exercise in the nude. My mother woke and tottered outside to witness the vigorous jumping jacks. Then, she told me, she sensed someone watching. When she looked, she saw a man's outline, half hidden by a tree. She approached him, and he said to her: "Little girl, please tell your mother something for me. All of my life I have wanted to see just two things—a naked woman, and a train—and now all I need to see is a train."

I had other favorites—how she and her brothers, for example, would open the back hatch of outhouses and poke their cousins' butts with long sticks, or the summer she acted as a human advertisement for a Swedish business (I don't remember which one) by water-skiing throughout Europe, one hand holding the speedboat's rope, the other gripping a flaming torch. I loved imagining, too, her brothers at play in the dense Swedish woods, even the most grizzly images: trapping long snakes with forked sticks and then throwing them onto hills of fire ants. My mother said the red ants could eat a snake in minutes. (Was Shakespeare's Gloucester correct when he proclaimed, "As flies to wanton boys are we to th' gods, / They kill us for their sport"?)

As a child, all I wanted were stories of her childhood. As an adult, I want to hear everything that followed. I am trying to remember my mother as she lived—in a stretch of time that now seems nearly detached from my life. My childhood memories blur into the early teenage years. Then, everything is severed absolutely: I am a kid, and then I am a young man. Two lives. In the first, a boy helps place candy on the roof of a gingerbread house. In the second, a man walks in the attic to seal the roof from rain or bats. In one, a boy climbs a towering oak to peer down at his parents' house. In the other, a man prunes dead limbs so they won't fall on strangers, or on his own children. The worlds seem as defined as rooms in a house, though in the first the door is now closed, and in the second it's open. In between: a room with boarded windows.

My father first arrived in New York City in 1948, after rejecting a lifetime position at the Philadelphia Museum of Art because he distrusted the director and knew he'd be manipulated. Instead, he accepted a job in animation for the Frederick House and rented an apartment at the top of the Broadway Central Hotel. Two years later, in 1950, he also rented a summer studio in Provincetown so that he could more easily study painting with his mentor, Hans Hofmann.

The studio had a large skylight—perfect light for painting—and was catty-corner to Hofmann's own home.

In 1956, however, several events took place that significantly altered my father's living arrangements. A group of about twenty-five people approached him about Hofmann's classes, announcing that the old man had decided to retire and requesting that my father take over in New York. My father knew he would require a larger loft and moved about a year later into a workable space located at Sixth Avenue and 24th Street. A year or two after that, he moved to a still larger loft on 25th.

The 25th Street loft, long since leveled for a parking lot that now features a weekly flea market, became the first home for my then-unmarried parents. The building had once been an old Vanderbilt mansion, but by 1959 its elegance had fully decayed. The loft had no heat and no hot water, but it had high ceilings and wraparound windows—ideal for an artist's studio—and somehow they managed to be comfortable. My father built a large platform out of wood that businesses had thrown out (this became the bedroom), and they depended on a thin metal woodstove for heat, primarily burning wooden cartons discarded by a neighboring import firm.

"At Christmas," my father explained as he retold some favorite stories, "I walked down the street to give the importers some money—a tip, you might say, for giving us heat. Halfway there, I ran into a couple of fellows who worked for the business, and they had money for *me*—you know, for hauling away their trash." Then he laughed and added: "The stove worked well at night, but by the morning, once the wood had burned, the loft was freezing. I used to feel pretty embarrassed, but Anita would wake up, stretch her arms wide, and say, 'Ah! *Fresh!*'"

My parents rented the loft on a month-to-month basis and one day returned to a note that announced the building's demolition. They would have to move in a month. So in 1960 they rented another loft at Fifth Avenue and 29th. That's where they lived for five years, constantly concerned about eviction since artists could rent lofts but were not allowed to live in them. From my birth, in 1963, until their last move, in 1965, I lived there, too.

But I'm getting too far ahead. Let me return to the summer of

1956. My father is painting in his Provincetown studio while his wife at that time, Barbara, works on her writing at a desk on the floor above. Someone knocks at the door: an attractive young woman who says she has heard wonderful things about his art classes and would like to study with him, but could he please give her work a brief critique? My father agrees, and she returns with several canvases. They talk at length, she thanks him profusely, and then she leaves. But a few minutes later, she knocks again and asks, somewhat sheepishly, whether he would be willing to critique her roommate's work as well.

"By now," my father used to explain, "I can hear Barbara upstairs, thumping on the floor because we're making too much noise, interrupting her thoughts. So I told this gal that we should perhaps go to their apartment instead. When we arrived, the roommate opened the door. I couldn't quite see her face because she had a large, floppy, straw hat that drooped down to her nose. She took out some of her paintings, and I talked a bit about them, and then she lifted the hat. And, oh boy . . . the sun came out."

That's how my parents met. A few weeks later, she began taking painting lessons with him, but the romance was not without complications. My father separated from Barbara, and they had an amicable divorce in 1959; they remained, in fact, close friends for the rest of their lives. My mother was also married at the time, not to an artist but to a businessman whom she now found terribly boring. (Her two weeks spent in Provincetown to study with Hofmann had been a treasured respite.) Though my mother and her husband formally separated in 1958, he refused her a divorce for four years, nor was divorce an easy procedure in New York because the person filing had to prove that the spouse had been physically or psychologically abusive. But my mother finally got his permission to proceed, and then she waited for the paperwork.

It's now the first week of June 1962. My parents have spent the morning packing their '58 Volvo station wagon in preparation for a summer on the Cape. The mail arrives: my mother's divorce papers.

"Wonderful!" she exclaims. "Now we can have a child!"

"Wait just one minute," my father says. "We're gonna get married first."

That afternoon, he runs around town to secure a Unitarian minister, and they get married the following morning. From the chapel, they walk to an old hotel for a celebratory brunch.

"Do you have some champagne?" my father asks. "We've just been married."

"I'm so sorry, sir," the waiter explains, "but I cannot serve alcohol on Sunday."

A few minutes later, however, he returns with bottles of ginger ale—a fancy brand with silver foil around the necks—which he has iced in buckets. With mocked sophistication, he pours the bubbling soda into two champagne glasses, and I love to imagine how my parents laughed, toasted their own good fortune, and, later that afternoon, relived the delightful humor of their celebration as they left the heat of Manhattan for the coast.

Sometimes, too, I enjoy imagining conversations that were not passed on to me—how my parents, for example, probably spent a considerable amount of time discussing parenthood as they drove to the Cape, having been married only a few hours earlier. I know my mother was eager to have a child, and my father, though forty-seven and fiercely independent, had agreed. Certainly, he would have warned her about various challenges—new financial responsibilities, the heightened risk of eviction from their loft, the fact that she would have less time to devote to her work—and certainly she would have cast the warnings to the sea. If a part of my father never forgot the treacherous boat rides that brought his family from Russia to America, their journey marked by bandits and wild weather and devastating financial losses, a part of my mother never let go of the flame she carried as she water-skied across the Mediterranean.

Whatever their conversation, this part of the story I know for sure: the following morning, my mother looked into the bedroom mirror and announced, "I'm pregnant."

"Don't get all worked up," my father said. "Sometimes it takes several months, even years." But she was insistent, because she understood the realities of her body far better than he could determine the odds.

"You know you're pregnant," she explained, "when your eyes turn the color of Swedish lakes."

# Transcriptions

Presumably, my father has just woken from a nap—having fallen asleep in front of us all—and asked whether I'm home, because at the start of the cassette I say, "Yeah, I'm right here," and someone else confirms ("He's right here"), and my father replies in self-mockery: "All right. Well then, go to sleep." There's laughter, and soon—with my eyes now closed to the intimacy of headphones—I can place the group: Thorpe, Bonnie, and Ashley; me and my grandmother; Pat and Lynne. It's Lynne who's brought the tape recorder and who may or may not have sent me a copy of the cassette before now, but, either way, I'm listening to this taped afternoon for the first time in twenty years.

Our friends tease my father for snoring, and my mother asks him, *Do you want us to stop talking?*

"No, darling," he replies. "I'm sleeping very soundly—according to my fan club." And indeed, he goes back to sleep, probably at the foot of the bed, his steady snoring a strange background music to an extraordinary afternoon.

It is April 12, 1980. Days earlier, my mother lived in a netherworld between dream and morphine-laden consciousness. By the next afternoon, she will be asleep for the night, and she will sleep all of the next day, until the hours drift into April 15, when she leaves our world.

But for these hours—or at least for these forty minutes—she's miraculously clear. She knows Thorpe and Bonnie and Ashley will return to Massachusetts by early evening, that this will be their final visit. And I do remember them leaving, how she told Thorpe, *We all get there at some point. I'm just going first.* But I don't remember the afternoon. At first, listening to the voices in mid-conversation, I feel conscious of the present: autumn, 2000. I'm thirty-seven years old. And then, in an unconscious dissolve, I'm seventeen again, and my mother is drawing on a will that's unimaginable to the living. With clarity and vividness, she speaks of her youth, while my father, who undoubtedly wanted to be part of the gathering, finally allows himself to rest.

He's already asleep as she begins the first story: my mother's in her early twenties and is on a train, returning to Sweden after several months working in Paris. The conductor walks through and requests passports. Only then does she learn that her passport should have been "stamped" (validated?) in France. He tells her she must have this taken care of when they reach the border at Belgium—that she can't continue her passage otherwise—but she has no money; she'd spent it all and had been living, in fact, on coffee and a bit of sugar. Fortunately, a Danish man in the same car needs a similar stamp, and he offers to lend her the cash. Even so, they have little time at the border and have to act very quickly.

*So we said, "Okay, we'll be ready there." And we had made some people . . . ready if we didn't make the stamp by three o'clock in our books. They would kick the luggage off the train*—[laughter of disbelief]—*and we would then stay in Belgium and try to* [appeal to the] *Belgian government and Swedish government and Danish . . .*

*So we then proceeded to wait. And, boy oh boy, they took their time, those conductors. They get excited for us; we'll all pee in our pants. Finally, they changed, and got the electric train—instead of the old steamer, or whatever they had—and inside all the French people had gotten off this train. All through the night: workmen, who started at three in the morning—four or five, you know—carrying sandwiches before they went to work. Marvelous peasants. The atmosphere was kind of wonderful and crazy.*

*In the last minute, they were tooting, and the cars started to roll, we got a piece of paper in our hands and jumped on, and we made the train.* [Again, amazed laughter—and you can almost see my grin when I say, "What timing."]

*It was unbelievable . . . They made it happen. Made it very, very scary for us.*

*Afterwards, I had been invited with this guy to have something to eat. He didn't have any money* [left] *and he was just . . . nibbling on something. And I was dying to know what he was nibbling on, but he didn't offer anything. Wasn't very generous, really.* [Laughter.] *He was very quiet. He was a sculptor, a Danish sculptor who had stayed in France for five months. Anyway, in the morning, there was a note, saying, "I know I can't go home with this to my mother—it's moldy cheese, and she'd kill me—and I think you might have wanted this. But it was too ugly looking; I couldn't offer it to you. Anyway, if you want it, take it; if not, throw it out." So, he gave me a big, round,* beautiful, *beautiful piece of cheese. Ugly as hell. But, boy, was it good.* [Laughter.] *Never tasted such rotten, tasty kind of cheese in your entire life.*

[Pat adds: "But it was like a piece of gold, you said."]

*Yes. It was like a piece of gold, it said in the book. In the book, it was like eating gold.*

What book could she have been talking about?

Upon first hearing that exchange, I stopped the tape and rewound the conversation, straining to make sure I had heard them correctly. I knew that the previous week, in a discussion recorded on side A of the same tape, my mother had conflated her bedridden present with a morphine-created reality. Speaking to Lynne, she had said, *Let's take a walk on Broadway,* and, for a moment, she *was* on Broadway, passing shops she knew well. In that same conversation, she mentioned a "book of life," as if everything had been recorded, like one's lifeline spun by the Norns: *I don't want to die . . . I really don't want to die. But in the book it says that it's coming. My book of life. My time . . . I'm needed someplace else.*

"Yes," I thought, "the book references must be connected." But later in the discussion from April 13, she asks Pat, *Was that part of the diary?* and Pat replies, "No. That wasn't in it." I had never heard of such a diary.

I telephoned Pat, now living in Washington State, but she could not recall the conversation, nor could she say whether this book actually existed. "It was such a difficult time," Pat said, "and I've forgotten a lot." Lynne had no recollection of a diary, either. My father did not know of one. Thorpe, other friends—it was a mystery.

And then my mind began to turn in on itself. I recalled the death of a well-known poet, a woman I knew, who had told her closest friend: "If I die before David, go through my journals and pull out the pages that will hurt him." Had Pat lied to me to save my feelings? Had there been a diary to *destroy*—one filled with incriminating stories that my mother wanted burned from record? What experiences could have scarred or embarrassed her so profoundly that she would make her dear friend lie about the evidence?

But if that were the case, why would she allude to such a diary when she knew—as I'm told she knew—of the cassette by her bedside?

In December 2000, I drove to New York in search of this diary, hoping for a discovery much like that of *Anders and the Norns*. But if the diary exists, I could not find it. The failure brought me back to the tape. It was Pat who had raised the topic with the words "you said" ("But it was like a piece of gold, you said"). Perhaps she simply knew the story, and my mother, drifting in a consciousness known only to the terminally ill, opened a spiritual "diary": the Book of Life. Then, later in the conversation, when my mother actually used the word *diary*, it's possible that Pat, overcome by the intensity of the moment, simply responded without fully hearing the question.

Although no friend could recall a written journal, each person, when asked, seemed struck by the suggestion of such an artifact. Most people, I think, find themselves intrigued by the archeological nature of psychology. Reflecting on people we've loved, we bring to memory so much of our own sensibilities and experience. Perhaps the beauty of artifact is simultaneously its greatest danger: the interpretation of what's been lost. Unburying the past, we can too easily bury our selves.

*I was the lucky one. I had the best jobs. I got this; I got that. I don't know how I got it. I was very lucky. Everything happened to fall into my hands. Not like my friend Ulla. She* never *had any luck.* [Laughter.] *She just had bad luck. That's all . . .*

This story had spun itself into the center of the first story, about the border crossing in Belgium. My mother had begun with the train trip, stopped with the conductor's reprimand, started the new story about Ulla (leading up to Ulla's engagement), and then concluded the train story. Untangling the two, Bonnie asked, "What happened after Ulla got engaged?"

*I had this incredible job* [in Paris] *where I was free at four o'clock. I just had to set the table for the family and eat with them, take the dishes out, and then come back for the people at night. When I got there in the afternoon—I'd been painting at school during the day, and learning French part of the day, and painting the rest of the time—I heard this noise. It was about one or two o'clock in the afternoon: "Oh! Ulla has gotten engaged!"*

*"Wonderful," I said. "Where are you going to be* [for the celebration]*?"*

*"We have no idea. We'll leave you a note at the Café du Dome and you'll find us."*

From here, my mother segues into a story of Ulla's past (a trip to the Riviera where she got horrifically sunburned), but the time shift throws her too far from the initial story about Ulla, and she's lost. My grandmother notices the slipping focus and, in Swedish, offers more details from the engagement party. An exchange in Swedish, then my mother switches to English: *Yeah, wait a minute,* as if to say, *Just give me a little time, Mom. I'll get to that part.* The group understands what she means and laughs.

At that point, I say, "She's doing fine here," and my voice has changed completely. It's obvious—and this amazes me now—that I am fully part of the experience, listening deeply, proud, maybe even delighted, mesmerized by the details. My grandmother immediately agrees ("*Ja,* she's doing fine"), and my mother begins again—*So, anyway . . .* —then feels lost—*Wrecked it now. I don't know where I was*—and Bonnie tries to prompt her, but something happens. Most likely, my mother spits up; a few seconds later, it sounds as though she wants help cleaning her mouth.

"You want some more milk?" Bonnie asks.

Almost inaudibly, my mother replies, *Nothing.*

Then I say, "Another one—" and Pat clarifies: "Another tissue."

"Boy," Bonnie says, "I'd be the worst nurse in the world."

There's a short amount of nervous, lighthearted discussion of Bonnie as a nurse, and then I redirect the conversation: "So you've got this note."

> *I've got this note, and when I got to the right place, they were sooo smashed.* [Laughter.] *There were two tables as long as this room. Our party; all belonged to our party. They were so drunk. They had everything on this menu that you could wish for. And I looked: there were caviar, the best kind of wines. Everything of the best you could dream, they had ordered. White wine, and wine rosé, and red wine, and back to this and whatever. It was supposed to be* the best wine. [In mock French accent:] *Ze best, you know. Best . . .*
>
> *I came for the dessert and champagne. No one could have the champagne. They were too drunk! There were glasses filled with cool champagne—only for me.* [Laughter.] *Just there waiting. They said, "We've saved you—well, here is yours."*
>
> *I said, "You're kidding." I was interested in what they'd eaten, what they'd done.*
>
> *There was dancing—a wild mess of everything—and then they said, "Who's paying for it?" "Well, we don't know."* [Wild laughter.] *Nobody knows who was paying for it.*

*Paul* [Ulla's fiancé] *had killed off everything he had before, in the Riviera, and he had no money. That was the crazy part of it. No one had a nickel.* [Laughter.]

[Bonnie: "What happened?"]

*We don't know. To this day, we do not know who paid that bill.*

And now everyone's roaring, cheering. When it dies down a bit, my mother continues with some subsequent stories: how Paul gets even more drunk and ties himself on top of a taxi cab; how Ulla becomes furious at his behavior; how they fight until he breaks off the engagement. Then my mother speaks of Ulla walking the streets at six in the morning—no place to go, no place to live—but my mother's getting tired, and the fluidity of her narrative deteriorates. There's the suggestion that Paul breaks things off from America. There's a brief mention of Ulla having TB, how no one wanted to hire her because of her cough. Later, we're told, Ulla leaves for America because my mother's there.

Headphones tight against my ears, I tilt my chair back. I've been laughing out loud and am smiling as my mother continues the story of Ulla, now in America: *The thing is, when she got here, I sponsored her papers—sponsored her, a fool—but—* I'm ready for the next adventure: Ulla bumbling through the streets of New York, perhaps, or taking a bus to the other coast. (Oh, how could I have forgotten that afternoon?) Wild scenarios jump-start and swell, but only for a moment, because at that syllable, the cassette spools to the clear leader, and she's gone.

Some fragments from that year I can relive too easily, though in most cases I never before had a sense of date, a sense of the timeline. I remember, for example, how this group of friends selected one painting each, but until I heard the tape I did not realize that the exchange took place three days before her death. Had I tried a little harder, I probably could have placed the moment close to that day, because the inscriptions on the back too honestly reflected her failing health.

Hands not steady. Vision doubled. My mother acknowledged the problems out loud while she penned her brief notes to her close friends. Now I see her gestures as heroic and beautiful, though at the time, when I watched the letters double and reverse—*Thaank you, for veerythinng*—my eyes kept returning to the carpet.

And suddenly I'm staring at the carpet again with my own double vision: it's within a week of my mother's death, and she asks Pat to sing "Summertime," with me accompanying her on my alto. That tape exists, too, but I can't bring myself to play through the whole song, and why should I? That memory has always been seared into my consciousness:

Pat begins the slow melody, pronouncing each lyric with a controlled vibrato and remarkably clear diction (she once sang on Broadway), and then I attempt to embellish the phrasing—but nothing's fluid. My lines sound either mechanical or bungled, my tone thin and edgy. Perhaps I couldn't navigate the key that suited Pat's voice; perhaps the answer's more obvious than that. But as she stoically pushes to the song's end, my fingers fail to find the tune's changes.

On tape, the mistakes sound that much worse, and when Pat sings, "Fish are jumping and the cotton is high," I hit the STOP button, then fast-forward through the performance, her voice and my saxophone now sounding like a special effect from a sci-fi flick. Did the tape keep running? Were there more stories here? I cue the cassette to the song's close. I can hear some people weeping, and then my mother speaks, her voice receding. She responds, I can only believe, more to the gesture than the musicality. She responds the way she did—almost exactly, now that I think of the words—when she received the foul-smelling cheese on that train from Belgium to Stockholm. She says, *Beautiful . . . just beautiful . . .*

Nothing else remains on that tape, but—another surprise—a little more remains in memory. Without knowing what I wanted to say, I turned to Pat and asked if she would come upstairs for a minute, and when we reached the second floor, I hugged her and wept. Except for one moment shortly after the initial diagnosis, this is the only memory I have of crying, for all those weeks. And I really sobbed. I must have turned my head into the crux of my right arm, because when I finally pulled away—and she held me for a long time—my sleeve had darkened almost to my wrist.

I never had a moment like that with my mother. In retrospect, I realize that was my choice, and hers as well. Years later, friends said she could not talk (at least not at length) about leaving me. She didn't fear death, but she could not bear to dwell on her separation from me. I guess we both decided that a formal goodbye wasn't possible. But she did manage to articulate her farewells to others. Although I do not recall being in the room when she spoke of Ulla and that threatening train ride, I remember vividly how she said good-bye to each person individually. *This is the way to go*, she said to Thorpe on the afternoon of April 13. *This is the way to do it*. And the following day, speaking to Lynne, before giving herself completely to sleep, she replayed the afternoon and, in doing so, replayed her own words: *It was glorious. Now I'm ready to go.*

# Lost Works

With the winter wind working its way through the broken pane and battered sill, the paint on the living room ceiling began to crawl and peel, so when my father and I walked into the Cape house in late May 1982, it looked as though hundreds of small white snakes had shed their skins. On the kitchen table, the intruder had mixed a variety of products that he had found in the basement (chemicals used for photography, canned molasses—who knows what else) and had written in the center of the gloppy mess: RUSSIA SUCKS. Then he grabbed a steak knife and walked upstairs into my room, where he opened the closet and a few drawers, found nothing of obvious value, and plunged the knife into a stereo speaker. In my father's bedroom, he gripped the base of a silver candelabra, which my father's family had managed to salvage when they emigrated from Russia in 1919, and threw it at the ceiling, probably several times, until the plaster gave way.

I could only interpret the knife in my speaker as a voodoo doll's pin. My father also assumed that the vandal had targeted us specifically. "Ah," he said, nodding slowly in the kitchen. "Someone's been told about my family and wants to make a statement." Various bottles of alcohol in the kitchen cabinet had not been touched. Drawers in my father's bedroom had not been ransacked for jewelry (though none existed). No, this was clearly a hate crime by someone who despised the damn commies and their jazz-loving children.

Or so it seemed at the time. Although we never pressed charges, and did not, in fact, have absolute proof, we figured out who broke in: our neighbor's grandson. The boy knew nothing about us, or at least nothing as personal as a family lineage, and we had been told very little about him. We were aware, however, that this boy's parents had never been able to control his unrelenting anger. In fact, a year before he vandalized our house, he had so outraged his father that the man literally screamed himself into a fatal heart attack.

We learned about the forced entry from a different neighbor, who walked around the property once or twice a week during the winter. At the back of the house, he discovered the broken window and, on the sill, a shucking knife that had been used to smash the pane. The discovery corresponded with this boy's visit to his grandparents' home, and, far more incriminating, the knife had been taken from their garage. We loved those neighbors, and although we showed them the knife, we did so with trepidation because we didn't want to damage the relationship. More than that, though, we wanted the boy to be heavily supervised should he visit again. He never did.

For the most part, the boy did not destroy invaluable items, particularly my parents' paintings, and the insurance company paid for the mundane losses. Even the candelabra had not been irreparably dented. So, somewhat bizarrely, we wove into our feelings of violation strands of relief. At each retelling of the story—and, naturally, we had to go through it numerous times with various friends—we concluded with some sentence that verged on gratitude: "It could have been so much worse."

But we lost two marionettes, one that my mother had made and one that she helped me create, and that loss tugged at us both. The face of my mother's puppet had a ballerina-like purity that perfectly complemented its puffy Victorian blouse. My marionette was more of a caricature, with a hooked nose and goofy '60s-hip attire. They had hung for years near the entryway, and though they were by no means the strongest pieces of art in the house, they nevertheless represented a sense of joy and whimsy that marked so many of my mother's projects. They also, I suppose, acted as icons for a mature mother and her youthful son. Where had the boy taken them?

Our neighbors spoke to his mother, who begged him to confess, but the boy insisted he had never gone near the house. We checked in closets and cabinets, and I spent many hours in the woods, imagining that he gripped the wooden crosses that secured the marionettes's strings and flung them into the branches. Sometimes I envisioned him cradling the backs of the papier-mâché skulls and smashing the faces again and again into a tree trunk until his hands turned white with powder. Could I have done the same to him—to *his* head—had he appeared during those walks? Wasn't it enough that he would spend the rest of his life knowing he had killed his father? I'd like to say I didn't house his rage, that this became a lesson in karma, but every fantasy of finding shattered puppets fused with visions of his pain: I wanted to tie him to a pine and force him to confess.

In 1970 or '71, when I was seven or eight, I asked my mother if I could write a letter to President Nixon regarding pollution in New York City, and she thought this was a great idea. I wrote several letters, in fact, and although my father intercepted a few ("They'll make a file on him, for crying out loud!"), others arrived at the White House, and once I actually got a reply, along with a subscription to *Ranger Rick* magazine. Even then I recognized the gift as a bribe, and as Manhattan's dirt and soot intensified, my letters became all the more direct:

Dear President Nixon,

Things are getting worse. Yesterday I could not stop coughing when I walked home from school. This should not happen! What are you going to do about it?

Sincerely,
    Sascha Feinstein

PS: My father didn't vote for you and my mother thinks you are a jerk. I think you are a jerk too. But please do something about the pollution.

Perhaps inspired by my passion and politics (and noting possible improvements regarding tact and erudition), my mother created a weaving that depicted the virulent nature of city pollution. Dramatically horizontal—six feet wide but only two-and-a-half feet tall—the weaving presents two related but antithetical scenes. The first consumes most of the space (about two-thirds) and portrays a queen, her arms angular and thrust overhead as she screams while an enormous snakelike dragon wraps itself around her king. The wide sun in the center and the bright earth suggest that this had been a beautiful land. But now a beast of smog and poisonous gas strangles the environment. In the background: a city of shadowed purple.

In the last third of the weaving, however, the king and queen stand arm in arm against a dazzling, golden wall. She holds bright flowers in full bloom, and he proudly wears a suit colored like the Caribbean. Perhaps my mother wanted this to represent the health of unadulterated countryside, or even the possible glory of city life, provided people could become more sensitive to urban disasters. I think it's also possible to interpret these scenes as body and soul, mortal jeopardy opposed to spiritual immortality.

Whatever her intent—and I suspect she would have welcomed various readings of this work, the most narrative of her career—she exhibited the piece in a large show in SoHo, along with many other weavings inspired by Scandinavian mythology. Most of my father's art students attended the opening of that show, and one invited her boss, Martin Segal, who had founded a national consulting and actuarial firm and later became New York City's first chairman of the Commission for Cultural Affairs. And it was Segal who focused on the pollution tapestry and purchased the work almost immediately.

I wanted to believe that it was meant for him. That he knew, somehow, the work would change his life. That he *had* to own it. (How can an artist, or someone who loves that artist's work, ever know such things?) When people speak of art openings, they tend to highlight sales as the mark of an artist's success, a comparison that fuses art and finance, and certainly those who create require a steady income just like anyone else. But I have rarely heard discussions about the sale of art as another form of loss, which might be a truer observation.

My parents documented the weaving before the show closed, and a fairly good reproduction exists in volume 23 of a Time/Life publication called *The Family Creative Workshop*. The article features my mother's tapestry work (how to start, basic technique, and so on) as well as a variety of applications: wall hangings, of course, but also pillow covers, window valences, puppets, handbags, and panels for decorative shirts and dresses. In one photograph, I'm sitting with my parents, the three of us modeling her handmade clothes. In another, I'm sitting beside a neighborhood boy to display woven hand puppets.

On the opposite page, my mother, father, and I sit on a wooden semi-spiral staircase that my father designed and constructed with curving hand supports that twist and groove much more like sculpture than merely functional architecture. We all look a bit self-conscious, especially my father, who's smiling his camera smile—working so hard to be natural. We're wearing clothes that incorporate woven panels, and I appear as cheery as an awkward twelve-year-old can look. I vaguely recall not wanting to be in the photograph and telling my mother so, and I can hear her saying, whether or not she actually said this at the time, "One day you'll understand why this is important."

Time/Life published *The Family Creative Workshop* series in 1976, roughly the same year that my mother drew a self-portrait based on a photograph my father had taken. I can almost envision the making of the piece, but, without question, I saw and photographed the completed drawing in 1986 and again in 1992, during visits to my grandmother's apartment in Sweden. In the original photograph taken by my father, my mother is smiling with her lips closed, looking more serene than anything else, and her hair is pulled behind one ear. She's lowered her head near a white rose of Sharon, and the flower's bright form startles the eye as though infused with moonlight.

In the drawing, she's taken out the flower and darkened the area near her chin. In fact, that part of the drawing seems *too* dark, not in keeping with the complete work, and—as I strain to analyze my four-by-six-inch photograph—it seems as though she's crisscrossed the flower into mere background, that she had sketched it and then felt the form too distracting in the new composition. Without the flower, her eyes transfix the viewer, the pupils dilated and emanating hair-thin pen lines darting to the edge of each iris.

For a show of my mother's work at the Cape Museum of Fine Arts in 2001, I wrote to my family in Sweden and, imagining this self-portrait as a marvelous greeting for the exhibition, asked them to mail the drawing. (By this time, my grandmother's health had declined dramatically so I could not contact her directly.) At first, they had no recollection of the portrait, which astonished me for all sorts of reasons, but they remembered the piece after I sent a duplicate print. At that point, I was sure they would find the drawing quickly because my grandmother's apartment, clean and orderly to the point of sterility, contrasted with my father's homes in all ways. But my uncles and cousins could not find the portrait. They opened all of her drawers and cabinets. They checked under beds. They searched their own apartments. They worked in teams and they worked individually, but, somehow, this rare self-portrait had vanished.

So we hung the show without that drawing and, in its place, framed a photograph in which my mother appears so strikingly vibrant that a woman who had never met her and knew our family only tangentially stared at it and wept. Still, I wanted to see that drawing on the wall and to know what had happened to the piece. Or to let go of the work. Or to be grateful, which I suppose I am, to have taken a photograph. And looking at my picture, I am lost in the unending interpretations of the self, as though I am watching my mother stand before a mirror that faces another mirror. All that remains from the lost work is a small photograph taken of a self-portrait drawn from a photograph for which she posed.

The original appears to be misplaced forever—could my grandmother possibly have thrown it out?—though I have uncovered enough not to believe in "forever." The marionettes also remain mysteriously lost, and I don't know what's become of that terrible boy, who's now a man, maybe somebody's father. But I recently discovered a photograph taken of a painting that my mother made, and in the still life she included her puppet. Ironically, we don't know where that painting is—in storage, or with a friend, perhaps—but I'm glad it exists somewhere.

As for the weaving about pollution, why did my father never tell me that Segal contacted him a few years later? I learned of this while we sorted through stacks of weavings in preparation for the large show at the Cape Museum. My father had opened bags of stored work, carefully revealing one piece after another. And there it was, the actual weaving: king and queen and virulent dragon.

Never in my life have I felt more caught between dream and reality. (Wasn't this exactly how a dream would unfold?) Martin Segal, my father explained, had moved to a significantly smaller apartment in the city and had little space for his art collection. "I could give the weaving to a museum or gallery," he said over the phone, "but I figured you would probably want it back." Like the work of art itself, the story abruptly changed from loss to complete recovery.

I wish I had a better sense of balance and design regarding what gets taken away and what arrives as a gift. It would be so much easier, and so less interesting, to base faith completely on chance or fate. Even now—right now, as these words fill the page—I find it somewhat unbelievable that the weaving hangs in my home, no longer relegated to a small reproduction in a slender book. What good fortune, and how beautiful to be sitting here this morning, drinking strong coffee and watching the sunlight blaze the windows of the turret in this Victorian house. Through the mottled panes of original glass, our yard's dappled like a watercolor, and I'm lost in fantasy, imagining an architect or mason in 1893 surveying the newly installed windows as the final half hour of light illuminates the interior, the oak floors now bright as dragon's breath.

And, oddly, it brings me back to the reproduction. I pull the volume from the shelf, open the text, and expect to stare at the copy, to compare the pale visuals to the vibrant image on the wall. Instead, I'm beautifully trapped in the photograph that introduces the Time/Life article: a full-page portrait of my mother working at the loom with our cat, Robin, sitting by her side, directly in front of a wide bowl of richly colored yarns, carefully selected and repositioned by the photographer. My mother is threading an aquamarine strand into the warp, and Robin is staring at the camera with that quintessentially catlike combination of wariness and warmth.

# Fire : Ceremony

Like too many rituals and sacred ceremonies in Bali, cremations have become something of an industry. The large advertisements along Kuta Beach look as subtle as billboards for Kentucky barbeque. Now, I'm told, tour buses clot the narrow avenues during the proceedings, but in 1987, when I first visited the island, the cremation I witnessed in no way seemed like an event for tourists. I felt honored to share in such a remarkable occasion, and my slides verify that I have not romanticized my experience: even when the images are thrown on a wide wall, it's challenging to find Westerners among the crowds. This is all the more surprising given the magnitude of that particular event. More than a year before I arrived, a high-caste member of the community had died, and, as is quite typical in Balinese culture, his family had postponed the service in order to prepare for the expensive, elaborate festivities. Other families had waited years to collect enough money and had very recently unburied their dead in order to share in this auspicious afternoon. Of the Brahman who died, one local said to me, "He was like king of the village. This will be big."

Those who have watched or read of a Balinese cremation will find my experience merely standard. The procession began in the village, with various family members carrying bones wrapped in white cotton and placing them within a pagoda-like tower (a *badé* or *wadeh*). Then a boy, perhaps a grandson of the deceased, climbed onto the structure and received wooden cages containing small local birds to be burned alive as escorts into the afterlife. And then he rose into the air with the whole tower, which I suddenly realized had been built on a wide bamboo platform designed to be lifted, dramatically, by many men. With one hand, the boy gripped a colorful umbrella, steadying himself and laughing as the procession shimmied perilously down the road.

Almost everyone, in fact, laughs or smiles at Balinese cremations; so much time elapses between death and ritual that the locals very naturally transform grief into celebration. I walked in the center of a nearly wild crowd until the thatched buildings thinned out and trees obscured any trace of a town. Deep in the woods, the boy on the tower helped retrieve the bones and offerings, and then the family replaced the remains within a finely decorated wooden bull (*lembu*), a magical coffin that only the wealthiest members of the society could afford. (Nine elaborate *lembu* stood magnificently beneath a single canopy. Other families—and over two hundred participated—had purchased less elaborate wooden representations; the poorest simply made wooden pyres.) I stood for a couple of hours, waiting for the various families to prepare for the event, or perhaps simply for the priests' appointed moment. Kids scurried through the crowd sellng coconut water and warm sodas. And then someone lit the bellies of the most intricately decorated *lembu,* and within two or three minutes every small area between the trees fogged and flickered like the actual ascension of two hundred souls.

Soon the crowd began to dissipate, except for those whose relatives had died quite recently and who therefore had to feed the flames to burn away the flesh remaining on the bones. Most others—even those who had been bankrupted preparing for this burst of fire—had no reason to linger. "To the Balinese," explains Miguel Covarrubias in *Island of Bali*, his famous study from 1937, "only the soul is really important, the body being simply an unclean object to be got rid of, about which there is no hysteria." Half a century later, my experience eerily paralleled his descriptions, including his passage on the aftermath: "The men in charge poke the corpses unceremoniously with long poles, adding debris from the towers, all the while joking and talking to the corpse. The crowd is neither affected nor touched by the weird sight of corpses bursting out of the half-burned coffins, becoming anxious only when the body is slow to burn. Soon the cow's legs give way and the coffin collapses, spilling burning flesh and calcinated bones over the fire until they are totally consumed." Some of the remaining ash gets covered with palm leaves; some gets collected and deposited in the sea. But the point of a Balinese cremation has much more to do with fire than ash.

How different from the Western world, where we expend so much energy on the burial of ash or flesh, and how unusual to remove grief from the rituals surrounding death. Standing as a witness in the flaming forest, I became so entranced by these unfamiliar rites that I initially made no comparisons to my culture, or even to my specific past. But later I thought about the ceremony for my mother, who wanted to be cremated and whose ashes we had spread seven summers earlier in Cape Cod Bay. My father chose the month of July, three months after her death, perhaps because he wanted warmer weather for the boat ride—or perhaps, like the Balinese, he knew only time would temper sadness. Whatever his reasoning, nature rewarded patience with glorious sunshine and blessedly low humidity.

The boat itself usually carried fishing expeditions and had more than enough room for the thirty or forty friends who boarded. The captain motored out just far enough so that the shore blended with the sky, and then my father began his eulogy, which we have on tape, his voice steady and penetrating against the rhythms of wind and water. Those words, public though they may have been, should probably remain in the private domain of husband and wife. But I can tell you how, after my father said good-bye, he tilted the urn into the wind, and then others threw flowers. As I wrote several years later:

>     Behind the large boat
>         lulled waves of lilies, roses
>
> from her garden sparkling the current,
>     and when a seabird circled the cluster
>         one close friend said she was with us.
>
> I don't know if I believed her,
>     but I watched the bird become a cloud
>         while the petals withdrew.

The flowers had been unexpected. My father and I had planned only on his eulogy and the scattering of ashes. But shortly before our guests departed for the boat, several women cut a few handfuls of stems from my mother's gardens—a lovely final gift, I thought. In a similar gesture, another friend brought onboard a bottle of Akvavit, which we poured into Dixie cups. Some tried sipping, but the strength of the alcohol burned through the cups' paraffin coating, spilling Akvavit onto the deck. It was almost as though my mother commanded from the heavens: "Oh, come on! Knock it back!"

What irritated and baffled me, though, were the two or three cigarettes that had been tossed overboard. The woman who threw them—a wonderful sculptor named Eleni—told my father, "At parties, Anita used to bum a smoke or two. I thought I'd give her a couple." Even now, the image of cigarettes floating with flowers repulses me: Marlboros unrolling in the current, the thin paper disintegrating even before, perhaps, it reached the sandy bed. But we all, I suppose, have to say good-bye in our own ways, and for Eleni, this had been her ceremony within a ceremony.

I threw nothing into the bay. I watched my father momentarily, before he vanished amid groups of friends, and when I looked back over the rail, I cried for the first time since April. I felt oddly stunned and embarrassed by my response, and then someone placed a hand on my shoulder: "Hey there, handsome." I quickly wiped my eyes, and she came into focus—Patricia, an old friend who had learned how to weave from my mother.

"Yeah," I said. "I bet I'm really good looking right now."

Then she pulled her fingers across my cheeks, drying whatever

I'd missed, and smiled. "Don't you know," she said, "tears from brown eyes don't streak."

---

Like many children, I first experienced death with the loss of a pet, not a person. In my case, it was my cat Robin, named after Robin Hood. My father, who preferred dogs, had insisted that owning a dog in New York City verged on cruelty, but when I turned four, a great age for begging, he agreed that we could get a cat. So that summer, not long after we arrived on the Cape, my mother marked ads in the local paper, and we left the house in search of a kitten.

Although relatively young at the time, I remember a great deal of that afternoon, especially one dilapidated house with overflowing garbage cans. We knocked several times before an enormous woman shuffled to the screen door and let us in. Greasy sauces had dripped down the stove, and I held my nose—right in front of this ogreish woman—before announcing, "It stinks in here!" The woman laughed in a breathy, restrained way, and my mother nervously asked to see her cats. The woman slowly pivoted towards the living room and whistled, and suddenly twenty or maybe even thirty cats jetted in from parts unseen and scrambled across the kitchen, some hissing and others screeching.

We did not stay to inspect them. (I think we were outside in a matter of seconds.) But at the next property, clean and bucolic, the owners offered my mother coffee while I played with a litter of five or six orange tabbies. Seeing that they had been cared for, if not pampered, my mother told me to take my time and choose any one that I liked. The kittens were chubby and playful—all except one, who looked thin and languid, and of course that's the one I chose.

"Are you sure?" my mother asked, over and over. "You can choose any one."

"I want him," I said, stroking the top of his head.

"That one over there is nice and round. Look at—"

"No, this is the one I want."

She had promised earlier that morning that I could make the final decision, and after several minutes of failed persuasion, we collected the litter's runt, and I held him on my lap for the ride home. My mother never asked me to explain why I selected the smallest and boniest of the bunch, but I could have told her: I thought his size meant he was the youngest, and that he would be the last to die.

Robin lived only eight years and in that time grew to be obscenely fat. In New York, he happily slept away most of the days, and on the Cape, though slightly more adventurous, he never developed any hunting capabilities. Other cats bullied him. Blue jays dive-bombed from the willow tree. Sometimes he miraculously landed on a mole and batted it around the lawn. In general, he had the nature of a big, gentle coward—and I couldn't imagine my life without him.

Although overweight and sluggish, he did not seem to be in any kind of mortal jeopardy, but when his body began to decline, it collapsed quickly and completely. Steadily and uncharacteristically, he began to meow in a high, awful pitch. We brought him to our vet and soon learned that his spleen and kidneys were failing. My parents explained that we would have to "put him to sleep," a phrase and a reality that made no sense to me, though I knew I had no options. The next day, I stayed home while they went to retrieve the body, wrapped in a black garbage bag.

We wanted to bury Robin on the property, and my father dug a hole near a tree that I had planted as a child. He made the hole extra deep so that raccoons wouldn't disturb the site. He also thought it would be better not to use the plastic bag but, rather, a cardboard box so that decomposition would take place more rapidly. My mother agreed and, perhaps thinking of Egyptian burials or simply in an effort to make me feel more involved, suggested I paint the cardboard sides. So I shared my mother's acrylic paints and brushed landscapes, I think, while she worked on large canvases.

We brought the multicolored box into the backyard, and I placed it at the bottom of the hole. My father got on his knees and angled the plastic bag until Robin's body slipped to the cardboard base. Then my father stood, and we all looked down. Not a sound. Finally, my mother said, "He looks like he's sleeping," and her voice cracked. That's when I turned my head and pressed it into her side. In my last memory of that day, my mother rubs my hair and says to my father, "He was trying so hard not to cry."

In the tiny universe of an individual Western family, birth and death tend to be celebrated only in the context of personal joy or grief. How many public holidays, for example, have retained the essence of their origins? Aren't we far more aware of dates that correspond with our selves? I was born on March 13, 1963, and, in a ridiculous and ridiculously American way, I used to scour jazz LPs to find a magnificent session recorded on the day of my birth. Blue Note records alone, after all, produced so many wonderful recordings from that year: Joe Henderson's *Page One* and *Our Thing*, Jackie McLean's *One Step Beyond* and *Destination Out*, Dexter Gordon's *Our Man in Paris*, Grant Green's *Idle Moments*, Grachan Moncur III's *Evolution*, Kenny Burrell's *Midnight Blue*, Lee Morgan's *The Sidewinder*, and so on. But no one recorded for Blue Note on my birthday.

The hunt was all ego, of course—jazz lover as Narcissus—but it's typical of human nature, I'd now like to believe, to self-aggrandize in that way ("I share a birthday with ——,"or "This house used to belong to ——," or, even more common, "I once ran into ——"). Ironically, the week of my birth coincided with events that took place halfway around world and that entailed death, not life. In March 1963, the Balinese had completed the first five months of Eka Dasa Rudra, a centennial ritual intended to coax gods into restoring the world's natural balance. The whole island makes sacrificial offerings, mostly concentrated at Besakih, their holiest temple, located on the slope of their largest volcano, Gunung Agung. Although a significant part of Eka Dasa Rudra had culminated on March 8, the Balinese had much to do before the next major event in April. And then, on March 12, Agung began to discharge mud and large stones.

Even though the smoke and the mud flows intensified over the next five days, no one, from what I've read, anticipated the magnitude of the explosion that ensued. Perhaps they felt protected by the intensity of Eka Dasa Rudra. Perhaps, with no witnesses living from Agung's previous eruption in 1843, no one could imagine such a reality. But when the volcano exploded on March 17, it killed over fifteen hundred Balinese. One young survivor named Sepek, who had been praying in a small village temple on the morning of the tragedy, described his experience to a translator for *National Geographic*:

"There was no noise at first, but then the *duk-duk-duk-duk-duk* of falling stones. Some people in the temple seemed to be sleeping. I tried to wake them, but they would not answer—they were dead. There were children, too, but they could not cry. They made strange wailing noises, because they had ashes in their mouths." Then the roof flamed and he ran for nine miles while ash speckled his body. "Fortunately," the article explains, "his wife and child had left Sorga two hours before the glowing cloud had come, and thus had been saved." Sepek saw this fortune as divine intervention—"The gods made them go"—but of the seventy worshipers who did not survive, did anyone claim that the gods selected them to die?

Of the numerous temples on the island, the most celebrated has always been Besakih, the central location for Eka Dasa Rudra. The temple did not escape thick layers of volcanic ash, and some of the architecture required substantive repair. But had it not been for the volcano's topographical channels—or had the gods intervened?—this stunning temple, with its black thatched pagodas directed to the heavens, would have been consumed absolutely by lava. When I visited Besakih in 1987, my guide told me about the explosion from 1963, but he never mentioned the fifteen hundred who perished. Instead, he spoke of the lava flow that spilled towards the temple and then split like a forked river in Hades, leaving the holy structure intact. "Besakih is our Mother Temple," he said to me, beaming. "She is a miracle."

I did not witness the men take my mother's body to the crematorium in Manhattan, and I was in school when my father picked up her ashes. I don't even know whether I tried to imagine what the crematorium looked like, or how much anyone is allowed to see. Nor did I have any interest in the ashes themselves, though I remember my father describing the blandness of the vessel provided: he said it looked like a tin can that had washed up from the Hudson River.

Maybe that's when he decided to make his own urn. He designed the shape, and later, when we arrived on the Cape, he asked his old friend Harry to reproduce it in clay. After the bisque, my father glazed the vase himself in a color he hoped would suggest a night sky, and then, with brush strokes that streaked like shooting stars, inscribed the urn with her name. I know he spent time practicing the lettering because I sometimes found napkins or scraps of paper on which he'd written my mother's name again and again.

The art of a kiln fire requires both expertise and good fortune. A single glaze often provides a great range of hues, even in the same load. Sometimes a particular glaze—blood red, say, or Chinese bronze—can fail a potter for years. Individual batches of clay also produce varied results. Although our friends at Scargo Pottery were as expert as anyone in the country, after opening the heavy door to the kiln that held my mother's urn, they discovered that some pots had cracked and some glazes had crawled or discolored. But the urn had been perfectly fired and emanated deep, luminous blues. No one thanked the gods, but, at that moment, I believe we all felt blessed.

During the making of the urn, my father and I planted a memorial tree, a copper beech that has since grown as tall as our house. We took turns digging the hole. I dragged a bag of peat moss from the front of the house, and he pulled a hose across the lawn. I remember that the planting took less time than I had imagined, and I felt almost startled when, abruptly, we had nothing more to do except to turn off the water, put our shovels away, and hope that the soil would sufficiently nourish the roots.

Several summers ago, during a visit with my wife and children, my son asked about the copper beech, because he knew we had planted the tree in memory of my mother and, at age six, had become more curious about death. We walked into the backyard when the afternoon sun charged the coppery sheen like the metallic iridescence of a raku glaze. My son stared for a moment and then touched a hanging branch.

"Do you see your mother's face in every leaf?" he asked.

I loved his question and wanted to tell him that I did, though that would have been a lie, and so I explained how I thought about the tree as a whole rather than as a collection of individual pieces.

"That's good," he said. "Otherwise you would be very sad when the leaves fall."

# On Angels and Demons

I held two part-time jobs the summer after my mother died, one at the Cape Playhouse, the other at the Cape Cinema. Neither involved any creative interaction with the arts. At the playhouse, I was the gardener, a position I occupied not because of my horticultural skills (which don't exist) but because I didn't need any. I'd arrive very early, water the plants and fruit trees surrounding the property, and leave before the senior employees arrived. I made minimum wage, but as a staff member I had free admittance to the shows, as well as to the green room, and that summer I met a great variety of actors and actresses, from starlets and heartthrobs to the wicked witch from Oz.

The playhouse director had just been hired that summer, and he tried to squeeze maximum energy out of everyone under his regime; by the end of June, he'd pissed off just about every employee, including me. He was a painfully nervous man, and I irritated him because I neglected to collect cigarette butts that had been flicked onto the lawn where audience members parked their cars. He wanted the butts collected daily but found me to be uninterested and unwilling.

Once, with a coffee can extended like a lantern, he ran through the lot and pecked at discarded smokes; I guess he hoped his chicken-without-a-head routine would guilt me into action: "Here's a butt, here's a butt, here's a butt . . ." I offered a mild, "Okay," but we both knew the reality of deadlock.

It's possible, too, that I took advantage of unspoken leverage. The senior staff, some of whom had been there for decades, knew I had spent the past nine months with a dying parent. Many had known my mother; others respected her professionally and knew her work, especially her paintings and weavings. Even those who had never met her, however, had been told that she'd died of cancer at the age of forty-seven. My adolescent antennae zoned in on my boss's nervous nature, and I must have realized that, no matter how irked he became, he would never find the courage to fire me over such pettiness.

At the Cape Cinema, I worked the concession stand and sometimes sold tickets. I'd pop the corn and try not to wince when I pumped the sticky ooze of fake butter. If someone arrived in a wheelchair, I'd open up a side entrance and help the person to a seat. Basically, I acted like a shortstop, fielding those in-between grounders and pop flies. But my boss was a gentle, beautiful woman named Lou Anne who treated me with respect, and her father played jazz trumpet—arguably the best trumpet player on the Cape. Given that particular time in my life, this seemed like a dream job.

The Cape Cinema itself remains a historic landmark, mainly because of the mural on its ceiling, a depiction of the heavens created in 1930 by the illustrator Rockwell Kent. "I was summoned by a Mrs. Edna B. Tweedy of New York," Kent wrote in his 1955 autobiography, *It's Me, O Lord*,

> to call upon her to discuss a possible commission to design and execute a large mural for a moving picture theatre at Denis [sic], on Cape Cod. . . . Intended for the elliptically vaulted ceiling of the theatre, its area would be 6,400 square feet and, therefore, "twice the size," as the prospectus of the theatre now informs me, "of Tintoretto's Paradise at the Doge's Palace, Venice, which formerly held the record as the world's largest canvas." I had a wonderful time at Mrs. Tweedy's, and her martinis were delicious; and after I'd had four—or was it five or six? —I said,

what was quite true, that of all the conceivable commissions that the world could offer I would choose hers.

The mural itself presented a swirl of celestial bodies—stars, yes, but also human bodies: enormous, naked figures soaring through the heavens. Kent included a large horse as well, this wingless Pegasus being my favorite creature in the panoramic display. By 1980, however, the ceiling had begun to peel, and peel badly. And, perhaps responding to the disrepair, audiences grew smaller and smaller. In a somewhat desperate attempt to raise more money, the cinema began to screen on the weekends a popular though utterly incongruous film: *The Rocky Horror Picture Show*. Almost every showing packed the house, and those attending grew wilder each week. As usual with showings of this cult classic, the interaction between film and its viewers became the central experience: they'd throw dry rice during the wedding scene, shoot water pistols when it rained, fling toast, unspool toilet paper ("Great Scott!"), and so on. Sometimes you would find abandoned cigarette lighters, newspapers, and the occasional rubber glove. For a movie theater with such historic dignity, the aftermath of *The Rocky Horror Picture Show* seemed grotesque.

The indignity seemed even more outrageous to me personally because on Saturday and Sunday mornings—the mornings free of playhouse duty—I cleaned the Cape Cinema. I wouldn't pick up a single cigarette butt for my other boss, but for Lou Anne, anything.

This was my routine: I'd bike to the cinema and open the front door. Inside, I'd unlatch all the side doors until the morning sun illuminated the entire theater. (This helped me see the disaster, as well as air out the stench of spilled soda and water-gunned candy.) I'd start with the restrooms in the basement, replacing supplies and mopping the floor, before confronting the theater itself. I'd walk the aisles and retrieve the largest pieces of trash (mainly toast), then haul out the industrial vacuum cleaner to suck up rice and wrappers. I'd adjust the white seat covers and replace those that had been stained. Then I'd walk to the front, stand on the elevated stage, and look down at the neat, white rows.

I'd leave somewhat satisfied, but I knew that in a few days (or hours) the wild ones would return, decked in costumes, often drunk, always ready to stain this landmark in the name of self-expression.

And though we tried to reduce the damage—"No butter on the toast," "No completely filled water guns," and so on—they bypassed all the rules. Had I been part of someone's group, perhaps I would have enjoyed the chain dances and lip-syncing. But I just shook my head as the loudspeakers doubled their frenzied choruses: *Let's do the Time Warp again! . . . Let's do the Time Warp again!*

---

Cut from the credits to the opening scene. An Indian chief hears from afar a spectacular soprano and falls in love. He commands his warriors to find the singer and bring her before him. Much chanting around the fire ensues, and then they're off to the woods, in pursuit of this magical songstress. When they finally find her, she has her back to the tribe, and since they drape her immediately, her identity is a mystery. She's brought before their chief and, still cloaked, she's commanded to sing. His smile says, *Yes, this is she.* But when she's unmasked, they discover she's monstrously ugly, and the whole tribe faints.

That was one movie my mother made with kids from the Cape during the summer workshops she taught. In another, I'm selling lemonade for the neighborhood, and my concession stand is wildly popular; no one has ever tasted such a spectacular refreshment. But when the drinks sell out, the camera follows me to the woods, where I urinate into the jugs. Cut back to the kids: they've changed colors! Dark purple. Scarlet. Bright orange. Some hold their hands up. Some dart their tongues back and forth in the gap left by lost front teeth. Collectively, they swarm like a dance of charming devils.

I thoroughly enjoyed these short films made with live participants, but the animated movies—the ones from a summer spent cutting out figures and objects that we'd drawn from numerous angles—captivated me still more. Yes, it often became tedious (in the age of computer graphics, it's easy to forget how many drawings were necessary for a few seconds of footage), and sometimes I became jealous of the attention that my mother gave to the other children in these workshops. ("They're paying for these classes," she'd say to me. "I have to help *them*.") But the solitary nature of these projects spoke to my sensibilities. I could work for hours without fading.

Of the eight or nine animated films we made that summer, I remember particularly well one about a pirate battle and one about balloonists. I made a curious movie that took place on the beach, where multicolored monsters emerge from the sands and tower over sunbathers before eating their bathing suits. Someone else made a still more risqué film that, as I recall, caused something of a stir at the end-of-the-summer screening: a giant chicken hatches human nudes—a man and a woman, who then fertilize some eggs of their own. The kids squealed and howled while their parents shifted awkwardly in the wooden folding chairs.

Sitting beneath Rockwell Kent's mural, the movie screen straight ahead, I sometimes daydreamed about those films. I also tried to understand why the mural didn't engage me more, why it seemed merely stylized. I'd stare at the heavens after cleaning the theater, following from form to form until the peeling ceiling almost became part of the fluid motion. How I wanted to connect my heart either to the myths or the motions. I owned Kent's illustrated text of *Moby Dick*, and I had a much greater affinity for those black-and-white etchings. Why did I feel so removed from these celestial forms?

After reading his autobiography several years later, I became less puzzled by my response; Kent himself clarified my emotional distancing. About the job proposal, Kent wrote:

> Of course I'd take it—but: I could no more consent to spend my life on the project than she could wait that long or pay for it. Therefore: I proposed that I design the mural and have others paint it; and that, with such a method or production in mind, I make it a design of so simple a character as to be virtually foolproof. And also—those martinis must have inspired me to quick thinking—that I would need, as an associate in the job, one who was experienced in the designing and production of stage sets; and that I would choose my friend Jo Mielziner. . . .
>
> The over-all design and detailed drawings of the figures were made by me. . . . The details of execution, terminating with the final installation of the mural in the Denis theatre, the so-named *Cape Cinema*, were handled entirely by Jo.

It didn't bother me that Mielziner had almost single-handedly installed Kent's vision of the heavens; after all, isn't it widely accepted that Tintoretto had others paint the majestic *Paradise* at the Doge's Palace? No, it was the nature of Kent's design: "so simple a character as to be virtually fool-proof." Given the hours I spent drawing and cutting out shapes for our animated movies, I should have understood what's obvious to me now: that Kent's etchings—the painstakingly scratched-out face of Ahab, or the side of the great ravaged whale—had more sweat and integrity than all the stars in that hemisphere.

Early in that summer season, it occurred to me that I could work to the accompaniment of music if I found the sound system, which I correctly assumed would be located in the projectionist's booth. I'd never been inside the booth, but I'd seen the projectionist himself emerge after the start of films. I discovered the door unlocked and climbed the steep stairs. The equipment—obviously outdated—looked like something from a poor science fiction flick, and I wondered about the heat in that small room, how it must have been unbearable in late July and August. But immediately, my attention focused on the turntable and the LPs stacked in the corner—mainly recordings by the Cape pianist Dave McKenna. I unsheathed McKenna's *Giant Strides* and walked downstairs as the standard "If Dreams Come True" arced across the vaulted ceiling and then through the aisles, out the opened side doors, and across the lawn. The music curved around the side of the cinema, and it woke up a man I'd never met before, a man who knew the music and followed the sound to its source.

"I'm sorry," I said, startled as he entered the theater. "We're closed."

"Oh, I know," he replied. "Don't worry," he added. "I live here. I'm Tim—a friend of Lou Anne's."

"You *live* here?"

"Yeah. Around the corner. Part of the building, actually."

I didn't believe him. For one, he looked like a homeless person: unshaven, wild hair, torn clothes, yellowed teeth. For another, I'd never seen anything approximating a bedroom in that building.

"Look," he said, reading my expression. "I'll show you."

We walked outside and around the back to an addition the size of a toolshed, one I'd never noticed. Within, I could see a mattress on the ground, as well as a large motionless dog and many empty vodka bottles. He said he used to date Lou Anne (something I also didn't believe but which she confirmed that evening) and that he used to play drums with her father. Now they'd split up, he'd lost his job and had no place to live, and she'd offered him this hovel.

"Don't get me wrong—I'm grateful," he said. "But it *is* weird living right here where she works, and not having a stove, and all that shit." The dog rolled over and made a sound that might've been a bark. "She's not doing so well, either."

I guess it was as close to a country-and-western tune as I'd ever witnessed: he'd lost the girl, lost the job, lived in a dump, and his dog was dying.

Once I got past the shock, however, I edited down his whole world; all that interested me were his experiences playing jazz. He'd been quite a solid drummer, I later learned, before alcohol overtook him, and he really knew the music. Some mornings, if I was still working by noon, he'd join me in the theater and we'd listen to records that I'd bring with me: Art Blakey, Max Roach with Clifford Brown—the stuff I knew he'd enjoy. I introduced him to my father, and Tim returned every so often to use our shower.

And then one day he left for his hometown in Florida—I think his family virtually kidnapped him in a desperate attempt to fight his suicidal alcoholism—and he didn't return. Not long afterwards, Lou Anne told me he'd gotten very, very ill and that he probably wasn't going to survive. It was the drinking, of course: his liver had given out, he'd turned yellow, and the doctors said it was only a matter of time. What I remember most is my steadfast refusal to believe that he would not regain his health, even after he slipped into a coma. I wrote to him in the hospital, and I wrote often. Sometimes I made felt-tip pen drawings on the cover of homemade cards. I don't remember my words exactly, just the swirls of color.

A week or two after Tim's departure, Lou Anne flew down to Florida. Tim's family had been told to gather; they'd gotten the call—"If you want to see him again, come now." And it was right about that point when Tim's body began to heal itself. No one knows how this happened, and I'm told he's in medical books. Cells reformed.

His body rehydrated. He woke to full consciousness and no brain damage. He put on some weight, gained his strength, and walked out of the hospital into a new life.

It's true that he collapsed a dozen years later—alcohol again: a failed marriage, other family problems, poor choices—but let me leave him in those years of recovery. Let me leave him sober, tanned, and handsome. In love. Father of a daughter who became the center of his world. Listening to tunes, maybe even playing. Yes, let me leave him there.

---

I've learned so much more about alcoholics since that strange summer. I've had a dear friend survive the addiction, another who didn't. And sometimes I think about my parents' fortunate temperance. My father used to drink mainly to induce a nap. His routine: random selection of cheap booze; long pull straight from the bottle; guttural response—*yuck*; and then: "Okay. Good night." My mother used to have a drink and a cigarette on Monday nights, when my father left to teach his art classes in Philadelphia. She'd usually invite a friend over, and her drink of choice was half an orange, squeezed, then left in the glass to soak in some bourbon. I loved the smell and often asked for the orange, which I never got.

A drink and a cigarette a week: hardly the kind of self-indulgence that causes death at forty-seven. Some angels and demons we create; others fly through our lives whether or not we desire their company. So I listen with tired ears to the monthly medical warnings. Nothing good is good for you, and if it's bad, give it time. Fat's now the main course of a popular diet. Wine's making a comeback. It's almost the holiday season—and all of a sudden, I'm reminded of my mother making glögg, the Scandinavian mulled wine: heated cabernet spiced with raisins, whole cloves, and cinnamon sticks. Just before serving, she'd splash Akvavit or vodka into the steaming pot, and then she'd fill pewter cups that quickly became almost too hot to touch.

She'd make glögg during the Christmas season and, once a year, carried a tray full of those metal cups downstairs into the cellar at the end of my father's Wednesday night art class. She'd sing "Santa

Lucia" as she descended the stairway, and my father joined the chorus once he heard her start. And some years, she'd wear a white dress and a crown of candles. When they finished their chorus, the class applauded and then, as the candles came into view, cheered, and I remember how he'd lift the crown from her head so her hair wouldn't burn, and how they kissed, and how we all toasted the coming year.

# Emerald Hummingbird

The hummingbird moth (a.k.a. hawk moth, sphinx moth, or sometimes common clearwing, as well as the corresponding Latinate names) resembles a hummingbird mainly because of its motion: it hovers over flowers while collecting nectar, its wings vibrating to a grayish blur. Some can be beautiful, like the zebra-patterned white-lined sphinx moth, but most tend to be boring brown with thin rusty stripes. Their bodies look fuzzy, somewhat like the skin of kiwi fruit, and they're small—just one to two inches long. Nor do they embody a hummingbird's graceful form; a hummingbird moth has a more uniformly thick body and two antennae that twirl together as they dip inside a flower. I've read a few statements arguing for the hummingbird moth's attractive attributes, but I'm far less generous. I think of it as the ugly cousin thrice removed. Dusty household moth to monarch butterfly—that kind of relationship.

Still, those who have never seen hummingbirds can easily misidentify these distant cousins, and that's what happened to my mother one summer. She saw a hummingbird moth on her phlox, and, having never seen an actual hummingbird on the Cape (and certainly not in Sweden or Manhattan), she thought she'd encountered the real thing. She ran into the house, grabbed her Nikkormat camera, unsnapped the leather protective casing as quickly as she could, ran back to the porch, and waited for the "hummingbird" to return.

This dash-and-sit scenario recurred several times during the summer. She kept telling neighbors and friends about her hummingbird, that one of these days she'd show them the camera's unquestionable proof of its existence in her gardens, but its sporadic visits rarely coincided with a camera-ready moment. Then one day the moth returned and didn't fly off immediately. My mother had no time to replace the 50mm lens already mounted on the camera body—a lens too wide for this kind of close photography—but she had enough poise to focus and shoot before the moth zipped along its invisible path. She finished the roll that afternoon and developed the film that evening. My father and I were warned not to go anywhere near the hanging strip of negatives, clipped and drying over the bathtub. You'd think she'd found the lost cylinder of Buddy Bolden's unrecorded trumpet.

The following night, in the hot attic that housed the enlarger, photographic paper, and chemicals, she made her black-and-white prints, and they floated in a small bath until the morning.

"*There*," she exclaimed over breakfast. "Do you see it? Right there."

I couldn't see a damn thing. My father brought out a magnifying glass. We said half-heartedly, "Oh . . . yeah," and she knew we were covering.

Then she offered some enlargements of the speeding brown body, but the shutter hadn't snapped fast enough to freeze the image, and this presumed hummingbird looked like mere shadow—a mush of tone against flower petals.

Other efforts yielded little more, but she became somewhat obsessed with this quest. She never stopped painting to sit in wait, but over lunch or during breaks she kept a keen eye on her flower beds. Her Nikkormat assumed its position near the screen door to the porch, and she made sure not to remove the 105mm lens, her best telephoto but one still not up to the job. And I began to resent this hummingbird, because every time she thought she'd been victorious, the roll of film had to be knocked off, which meant I had to pose, and I hated posing.

"You don't like this now," she'd say, every time, "but you'll be grateful for these photographs when you're older. I promise."

What kid imagines nostalgia for childhood? *Sure, Mom,* I thought as I smiled poorly in front of snapdragons and iris, or beneath cedar trees. Spoken out loud, the expected polyphony:

"How many more?"

"Just a few."

"One?"

"Be patient—and move a bit that way so I can see the garden."

"Come on, Mom."

"Stand straight so we can see how tall you are."

"*Please*. I want to go play."

"All right, all right, all right—go."

I'm not sure when, exactly, she captured the image of the hummingbird moth, or who told her the truth about its identity. But I do remember laughing about it with my father. (Guys love to wear cruel shoes and often taunt before they think.) We laughed and laughed, never pausing to consider the obvious: it may not have been a vibrantly colored hummingbird, but what difference would that make, anyway, in a black-and-white photograph? She had waited patiently and finally caught on film something magically fast, something that could hold itself stone-still in the air. How big we thought we were, and now, refocusing, how small.

I became somewhat serious about photography a couple of years after she died. Soon thereafter, I found her Nikkormat and, in 1987, took it on my first trip to Indonesia. I loved the old Nikkor lenses, rose-tinted and sharper, I liked to believe, than the newer Nikon equivalents. But somewhere on the train from Jakarta to Bandung, the camera broke inside my new camera bag. How this could have happened I'll never know. I leaned out the train window to quickly frame a portrait of children selling coconuts and colored fans, and suddenly the light meter began to quiver like a seismograph reading. A new battery: no change. Then I tried to switch lenses, but the bayonet mount refused to twist them into place. For a long time, I simply stared at my bag filled with accessories and thirty rolls of Ektachrome. Terraced rice fields passed my window in a blur.

I had been staying in Singapore with the family of my future in-laws and had flown into Jakarta an hour and a half before boarding the train. With only two weeks to spend in Indonesia, I had planned a fairly tight itinerary: a train ride to Bandung to hike in the volcano and see the countryside, another train to Yogyakarta for the ancient temples, then a flight to Bali. I had no fear of traveling alone, but in my first hour—bargaining for a taxi from one station to the next, bobbing in a ticket line as though riding waves in a sea—I realized that the energy of Indonesia far surpassed my naïve, preconjured imagery. Faces, temples, rice fields—the photographs had developed in my mind long before I took them.

And I brooded about that as I waited to arrive at my first destination. At every glance out the window, I witnessed miraculous landscapes. At every train stop, reaching towards passengers, beautiful old hands offered bright bananas and purple mangosteens. I knew my father would never travel to Southeast Asia, and I wanted to share what I had witnessed, but the memories already seemed lost.

The train station in Bandung was only slightly less hectic than the one in Jakarta. Here, too, hoards of locals elbowed forward to help the foreigners who clearly did not know the area. As if skin color wasn't enough, my straw hat marked me as a guy who couldn't tolerate the equatorial sun, and my camera bag let them know I had bucks. (The exchange rate during my trip was over 1,600 rupiah per US dollar. A full meal cost about fifty cents.) My tour book guided me to a fine, inexpensive hotel, where I checked in. It was four in the afternoon, a Saturday, and I asked the front desk where I might find a camera shop. They circled a street on my map of the town. From what I could see, the store didn't seem too far away.

But a combination of absent street signs and miscommunication with people along the road kept me from locating the store for quite some time. In fact, I came across it almost by chance, since a trishaw driver and a woman collecting cardboard hid much of the entrance.

Inside, Nikons dangled from the walls, and I explained with my hands that my camera had stopped functioning. They called into the back room for a clerk who presumably spoke English. His message could not have been more emphatic—"No, no repair"—but he did scrawl directions with a snaking line leading towards a large X.

Strangely enough, his cursive line drawing was easier to follow than my fairly detailed map. I walked past the main street and along several potholed roads where dirt kept spiraling from bicycles and a menagerie of animals. Soon I found myself checking for the right house number, and soon after that I knocked on the door of a small home. I wanted the impossible: someone who could speak English and who could fix my problems by the following day—a Sunday.

The man who answered looked Chinese Indonesian, though his skin color and eyes were somewhat Caucasian, suggesting a Dutch influence as well. He smiled, bent his head. I stepped forward and, holding up the Nikkormat in preparation for more hand signals, asked in the slow drone of an already-judgmental foreigner: "Do you repair cameras?"

He looked at me briefly. "Yes, yes," he said. "Yes, come in."

Inside, dark shelves lined each wall from the rug to low ceiling, and on each shelf, packed together like the remains of a massive war of tiny iron soldiers, a toystore's worth of trinkets choked every possible bit of space. On one wall, the centerpiece was a black-and-white poster of an American soldier in Vietnam, with big letters in the corner asking, WHY? The dark green couch by the door seemed more like an undulating piece of sculpture, and the oval wooden table in the middle of the front room tilted noticeably from right to left. He pulled over a chair for himself and motioned for me to make myself comfortable within the couch.

"I think I know what's wrong," I told him, and as I explained my educated guess he slowly turned the camera in his hands, listening, apparently understanding. When I had finished, he shook his head and said quickly, "No." I pursed my lips, then looked aside. He tried to explain to me the mechanics, what needed to be done. I had no choice but to trust him, though I didn't entirely.

"So it's possible to fix it then?" I asked, gesturing with my eyes and hands.

*Emerald Hummingbird*

"Maybe," he said. "I hope so. I can never tell until I go inside."

I gave him the name of my hotel and the room number, and only then did I realize we hadn't introduced ourselves. I told him my name and extended my hand. Then I asked for his name, consciously focusing on his mouth. I said to myself, "You *will* remember his name. No matter how unusual and complicated, you will remember it." He shook my hand firmly.

"Good to meet you," he said. "My name is Harry."

He told me to come back the next day at around 3:30, and I walked back to my hotel knowing only that I had no options. I could not afford a new camera, nor did I have time to look for a repair shop at my next destination, Yogyakarta, before visiting Borobudur, the primary reason for my entire Indonesian trip. How could I possibly see Borobudur without my camera? I ached, and that evening I wrote this embarrassingly overdramatic oath in my journal: "If this camera gets fixed, I swear to recognize the *energy* in what I see and not accept the image for the soul."

The following afternoon, I retraced my steps to Harry's house. He opened the door. I looked into his eyes and asked quietly, "Could you fix it?"

"Oh yes," he said. "Exactly what I thought. All fixed."

My eyes closed—"You're a *genius*," I said—and then Harry laughed and asked me in for tea. Once in the living room, he gave me the camera, and I checked the light meter, watching it balance to every nuance of shadow. His daughter Esther brought a tray with a clay teapot and sweet biscuits, and we talked about photography, and Indonesia, and America. We talked about family—his wife had died unexpectedly and he was saving money to send Esther to college—and to my surprise we talked until the sun went down. Then I paid him much more than he asked, shook his hand again, wished his daughter the best of luck, and waved back as they waved from their doorway.

About a block later, a couple of children emerged from the trees along the side of the dusty road. One smiled, and the other asked, "American?"

"Yes," I said. "I'm from America."

They laughed, and the boy who'd spoken yelled, "American!"

Then other kids ran to the center of the street. I clutched my camera bag tight to my side but soon eased my grip. One boy held out his hand to brush my swinging palm, then another did the same, and then a couple of girls walked to my side. They giggled as fingers brushed across fingers. We kept touching palms and fingers, fingers and palms, as I walked down the road, and when it was clear I had to travel beyond their part of town, they stopped and waved and danced. They whistled and laughed, their shadows dancing in the rising evening dust.

My experience in Bandung took place two years after a memorial show of my mother's paintings and weavings. An old family friend and great potter—whose name is also Harry—asked to have the show in his gallery at the Scargo Stoneware Pottery, an oasis of sorts in the midst of Cape Cod pines. My father set terms well in advance of the show: "Nothing will be for sale. Nothing." And Harry very agreeably accepted. So in the summer of 1985, filling the interior gallery and the outdoor exhibition space (well protected by a plexiglass roof but open to the air), we hung about thirty-five works. They ranged in size from ten square inches to six square feet, and they illuminated the walls with a symphonic radiance.

 The turnoff for Scargo Stoneware Pottery is easy to miss. If you're heading down the Cape on Route 6A, you'll enter Dennis and wind through the town, past the Public Market and the large cemetery and the post office. After a conglomerate of chintzy antique shops and cutesy eateries, 6A curves and rises over a hill. Immediately afterwards, the road forks, and if you concentrate on the bend or the split, you won't notice the pottery's sign—made from stoneware—above a perpendicular road that makes a steep descent to Scargo Lake. Plenty of people drive on by.

 And plenty of others don't. I've never seen the pottery empty, and for decades the biggest challenge for Harry and the other potters has been to produce enough work to satisfy the demand. Visitors turn off 6A, drive slowly down Dr. Lord's Road, see Scargo Lake to the right and another pottery sign to the left, and make a short ascent within the small forest of pine trees. And in a minute, when the drive levels out, the galleries appear and, among the trees and gardens and baskets of brilliant flowers, the art itself begins its show: carved sea-blue bowls and scarlet vases, clear-glazed porcelain and iridescent raku, the stoneware castle at the center of a fishpond and other clay castles filled with sunflowers for excited chickadees and sparrows. Visitors say, "Fantastic." They say, "I've never seen such a place." They say, "My God."

In my childhood, I could happily spend hours a day at the pottery, the way my children do now when we visit. Sometimes I worked in clay; sometimes I explored the woods; sometimes I just sat and watched Harry throw pots, my eyes unfailingly entranced by the metamorphosis of clay. I'd watch him lean into a large mound of flameware or porcelain, compress the clay to eliminate air pockets, then center the entire conical wedge on a wheel and make form after form after form. Swan-shaped wine decanters. Large wedding plates. Teapots with perforated inserts for tea leaves. He'd fill shelves with drying pots, and other shelves with pieces cooling from the kiln; still other artists, in both galleries, displayed work recently completed, with the promise of more to come.

My mother, no surprise, loved the pottery, too, so it seemed exactly right to have her show there. The interior gallery featured a combination of her abstract paintings and weavings. On one wall, for example, her weaving *Asgard*, named after the Norse kingdom, hung near an acrylic painting that featured similar blue tones, the two separated by a thin, vertical, bright red tapestry. One small weaving—the most obviously narrative in terms of realistic imagery—presented an Edenic portrait of a woman in a white dress beside a tree over-fruiting with apples.

In the vitality of natural light, the paintings outside became that much more expansive in gesture and dramatic in color. One particularly large canvas, roughly five by six feet, poured forth with such a planetary red—the red within deep red, the *essence* of red—that many viewers walked right by the black-and-white photograph of my mother, as well as the framed biographical statement written by my father. His essay spoke of her education and accomplishments, but more moving and insightful were his statements about her art.

He explained how the imagery from the weavings often evolved from Scandinavian mythology. "The paintings," he continued, "while emerging from similar origins, are also conditioned by Anita's deep love for the ordered wildness of nature, by elemental rather than cultivated aspects of her surroundings, and by a spirit in mystical connection with sources beyond surface appearances." In the next paragraph, he wrote:

> Anita Askild's paintings are characterized by strikingly rich colors and an emotionally charged intensity that conveys poetic overtones of environmental experiences in her native Sweden and in this country. Song-like, they range from dark, brooding qualities to sunny, light-hearted gaiety. Always they are forthright human emanations that extend the endearing candor of Anita's own nature. Their warmth engages the observer in immediate rapport; whether quietly somber or exuberant with the energies she sensed in nature, Anita's paintings take us into a direct sharing of her vision even as we enjoy her pictorial translation of it.

I documented the show with color slides and, projected against a wide screen or white wall, they approximate the experience, though slides are obviously no substitute for originals, nor can a projected image capture the other sensory impressions that were so much part of the experience: the smell of pine, say, or the music of Ravi Shankar floating from the stereo in the pottery. Nor do I have any photographs of us hanging the show, because I helped hold the large canvases while Harry's children and apprentices worked swiftly with hooks and metal wires, balancing and centering each piece. And that's when this happened.

We had almost completed the hanging and, in fact, had only one large canvas left to go. It was a vertical piece, about three feet by five, with an explosive lavender core, darkest at the painting's base and then spreading towards and across the top left-hand corner. Pushed to the sides: blues and greens from an ocean lit simultaneously by sunshine and starlight. Or was this the illuminated atmosphere from an astonishing, combustive galaxy yet to be discovered? Genesis. Resurrection. Atlantic, Atlantis. Doesn't the actuality of abstraction yield to the absolute reality of abstract truths?

I held the base of this canvas while an assistant on a ladder secured the painting on the wall—and suddenly he whispered, *Don't move*, and lifted his chin just enough to direct my eyes. To his right, above his shoulder and seemingly mesmerized by the painting itself: an emerald-bellied hummingbird. Deceptively motionless, as if challenging the Earth's gravity, it radiated like a jewel with the last of the sun.

Several people later told me that hummingbirds had never been seen before at the pottery, and this one kept returning to the outdoor gallery for the rest of that late afternoon. Right until dark, hand gestures: *Over there*. The potters didn't know the history of my mother and her "hummingbird," but they'd known my mother, and that was enough to leave them without language.

# In Honor of the Sacred Heart

For several decades, before it was loaned to the Tate Gallery, then to the Hirschl & Adler in New York, and later sold to private owners in Texas, the marble sculpture of Ezra Pound's head stared over a stone terrace in Tirol, Italy. The marble was the only large piece of stone that Henri Gaudier-Brzeska ever owned—Pound had purchased it for him—and it was the largest piece he ever carved before dying at the age of twenty-three from a stray bullet fired in World War I. I discovered Gaudier during the year of my mother's illness, a time when the arts acted as both sustenance and distraction. I spent most afternoons playing the saxophone. Some evenings I heard music, and other nights I watched movies at the Thalia, where I saw *Black Orpheus* for the first time, returning every night of its showing. On weekends, I often walked to galleries, and one day I asked a curator at the Museum of Modern Art to take me to the storage area where they kept Gaudier's magnificent *Birds Erect*. I read and reread Pound's *Memoir* for Gaudier and began to appreciate the extent of the poet's unresolved fury. "It is part of the war waste," he wrote. "A great spirit has been among us, and a great artist is gone."

But the reproductions of Gaudier's sculpture that appear in *Memoir* inspired me more than they evoked the pathos of his death. His pieces reminded me of jazz improvisations, stone carved into marvelously jagged flights of movement. Those images stayed with me, and when I graduated from college, I bought Pound's *Memoir* because I needed to own it. I found a copy downtown at the now-defunct Phoenix Bookstore, where I knew the owner, Robert Wilson. When I told him of my summer plans to travel in Europe, he suggested I telephone Pound's daughter, Mary de Rachewiltz, if I found myself in northern Italy, near the town of Tirol. "I met her at a book sale in England," he said, "and I imagine she must still have a good deal of Gaudier's work." I wrote her name down on the sales receipt and put it in my wallet next to a fortune that I'd saved from a Chinese dinner, a misprinted fragment that read, "You will." A month later, alto saxophone in hand, I left the country.

That's when I went to Sweden—that first trip after my mother's death—staying for two weeks before heading south. The nuclear power plant at Chernobyl had exploded a few days before my arrival, and everyone, city to city, felt vulnerable, if not panicked. Scandinavians and Germans kept testing their lakes for radiation, and the results proved that the Russians had not fully disclosed the magnitude of this disaster. Still, I refused to be alarmed. I played music in Denmark and Hamburg, in Amsterdam and Antwerp, through southern France and into Italy. I played in crowded parks and empty piazzas. If fate stirred winds to poison my breath, I at least blew away what I could.

And when I arrived in Verona, roughly 120 miles south of Tirol, I remembered to call Ezra Pound's daughter, because I'd been unable to stop thinking about Gaudier. Somewhere in northern Europe—East Berlin perhaps—I realized I was the same age that Gaudier had been when he was shot, and somehow this intensified my desire to see his work. For forty minutes, however, I failed to get the telephone number out of directory assistance. "Do you speak English?" I asked.

"Yes. A little."

"I need information for Tirol. De Rachewiltz. D-E-R . . ."

"No. We don't have."
"Please, let me finish: D-E . . ."
"You call back at four, okay?"
"Just one minute. Just try, please, for one more minute."
"Maybe you call back at four. I think it's best."

I kept thinking of Gaudier's sculpture, and about my mother, who told me always to take chances, not to have regrets. And I don't know how this happened, but suddenly a different operator came on the line, and she gave me the number I needed.

It worked. I nervously introduced myself, and Mary de Rachewiltz graciously invited me to come the following morning. "It's quite easy to get here," she said, but in point of fact it took the better part of a whole day: two buses, a train, another bus, and finally a short walk. When I reached the top of a hill, I saw an enormous stone castle, Schlöss Brunnenburg, to which Pound returned after his twelve-year incarceration at St. Elizabeths Hospital. In the foreground, lush vineyards cascaded towards the valley, so richly green that they seemed to reflect the hues of the surrounding mountains. Blinking from the sunlight, I walked the dirt road that twisted towards the castle. I didn't know how I could possibly return to Verona that day—the trip had taken too long—but I didn't care, either. I would sleep under the grapes if I had to. I felt like Orpheus in the film, before he loses Eurydice—when, dressed in his gold Carnival costume, he dances down the mountain, a huge kite of the sun glittering overhead.

With the 1998 Brazilian release of *Orfeu*—an adaptation of the play *Orfeu da Conceição*, on which *Black Orpheus* is also based—it has become politically unfashionable to admit a love for Marcel Camus's 1959 classic. The Brazilians apparently felt from the start that Camus had appropriated their land and manipulated their people for his own purposes and that the film did not speak for Brazil. (If this is indeed a fitting dismissal of the movie, then perhaps Camus should be criticized for appropriating Greek culture as well, the way Ezra Pound, some might argue, appropriated Chinese culture in his modern translations.) It had never occurred to me that anyone could respond negatively to *Black Orpheus*, much less do so with such personal hatred, and the reaction still baffles me.

I first saw the movie at the Thalia, a revival house formerly located on 95th Street, with an atmosphere that always added to the romance of foreign films, and to the intensity of this particular one. In 1931, two entrepreneurs had transformed the Sunken Garden Restaurant into a theater, which eventually became a Manhattan landmark. (In *Annie Hall,* Woody Allen's final encounter with Diane Keaton takes place outside the theater, but you'd need to be a New Yorker to notice.) From the outside, it never looked terribly special. Inside, however, the Thalia retained the sunken garden feel; beneath street level and poorly lit, the movie house felt almost Dantean.

Before experiencing *Black Orpheus*, I had relegated mythology to textbooks. But all of a sudden, set in the context of Carnival and imbued with tropical colors and Brazilian music and dance, mythology came to life. The images and sounds of Carnival replayed in my mind for months. Orpheus tossing an orange in front of a swash of blue. Eurydice unveiling herself until his whole world becomes her smile. The skeletal figure of Death leaping faster than a switchblade through the surreal festivities. And that sweet close, where, I'd later write, "boys just young enough / to dance into belief / pull the sun to morning / with solo guitar and samba."

But perhaps more than anything else, I reflected on a scene that takes place after the dancing and the chaotic chase, after Death tricks Orpheus into electrocuting Eurydice, very shortly after Orpheus wakes to what he thinks must be a nightmare. A police officer, not knowing what has taken place, asks him to perform again, to demonstrate the footwork of his dance—"You know, the one that you did at Carnival. Something like this . . ."—but he's speaking to a man who's as dead as a live man can be. No response, so the officer sends Orpheus into the night, towards the Missing Persons Bureau, where he takes an elevator to the twelfth floor. He exits onto a hallway—dark and empty, the way I remember my mother's ward at Columbia Presbyterian—and each quiet step casts a terrible echo before he calls for assistance.

He's still wearing the gold suit from Carnival, the top crisscrossing his chest and the bottom something like the chain-mail skirts of Greek warriors, though the metal looks more like the scales of a fish. He encounters a custodian who's sweeping reams of paper fluttering from rooms that line the landing. "You won't find any missing persons in here," he tells Orpheus. "All you'll find is paper."

Orpheus walks into one of the rooms and encounters stacks upon stacks of papers, the top ones curling, even the center papers curling. Obviously, no one has ever looked through them; they simply rise from the floor and desk. And the fans keep lifting them so that they float around within the room and into the hallway, and then the custodian sweeps them up and throws them God knows where.

He tells Orpheus that the building is stuffed with these papers, floor after floor, room after room. "It's all paper," he says, trying to prove that there's nothing else, adding, "Can you read?"

"Yes," replies Orpheus.

"I cannot," he says.

The custodian tells him to go into a room—"Have a look. See for yourself. There's nothing here. There are only papers here."—and Orpheus follows his suggestions. He walks into the room and turns within the pillars of paperwork. He knows that what he's been told is the truth, and before he walks out of the room, he holds the doorjamb with one hand, drawing the other from his eyes to his chin. It's a gesture that takes over his whole body, one I'll never forget, because we enter his consciousness entirely: *I have many, many things I need to do now, but I have no idea what they are. I know grief. I know loss. But I don't trust grief or loss. This is not the answer, but there must be some other answer. There* must *be some other answer, but I don't know where to go. I thought for sure I would find her here, that she'd be here among all these papers, in this home for the lost . . . I was wrong.*

The custodian tells him he must call for her and takes him out of the building to a meeting place—a room of witchcraft and chanting and spirit channeling, where Eurydice momentarily inhabits the body of a stranger. But before they get to that point, even before they encounter the dog Cerberus barking at the metal gate, they walk down the spiral staircase from the twelfth-floor landing. It's photographed from above so that they appear to be inside a massive conch shell. Their steady footsteps echo within the chasm of this stairwell, its center utterly black except for the occasional scrap of paper floating across the expanse, each sheet isolated from the others and descending more slowly than the last leaves of autumn.

---

At the iron gates of Pound's castle, Mary de Rachewiltz herself greeted me warmly and invited me in. She was tall and elegant and had a bun of gray hair pristinely pinned. She explained that I could of course see the Gaudier statues but that she would have no time to show me around the grounds. Inside, she introduced me to her husband, Boris, a man with a neatly trimmed beard who was translating *The Book of the Dead*. He asked me about my profession, but I really didn't have any satisfying answers. I'd just finished college, I was headed for Bloomington, Indiana, to do graduate work in English, I hadn't established myself in any field, and it was clear from their inflections ("Oh, I see") that they had no title for me, no label—not quite a writer, not quite a musician.

But they were polite and began pointing out the various collections of other members of the family: Egyptian masks lining one wall, Chinese stoves, shelves of smoking pipes, a glass table filled with scarabs. Then we entered a room filled exclusively with books by or about Ezra Pound, and I asked if I could see the original *Memoir* that he wrote for Gaudier. She insisted on turning the pages herself. I felt very humbled by the reproductions—so much sharper than in my paperback—and said something obvious about his youth and his genius. "Yes," she agreed. "It is lucky that there are very few Gaudiers in this world or we would all feel miserable about ourselves."

She then showed me Gaudier's marble cat, a relief carved into a broken stone, brilliantly manipulated into the animal's curve. She said there were days she felt guilty that more people could not enjoy the work she owned and handed the cat to me. I felt his engraved signature on the bottom, pulled my fingers across the subtle folds of the form. In my mind, I could still feel that stone as we walked through the castle.

When we reached a room hung with large photographs of Pound, she suddenly asked whether I would like to stay overnight in the guest house—a large, wooden cabin situated not far from the castle. I could choose any room that suited me; a group of scholars had canceled their visit because of Chernobyl, and so, she said, it really would be no problem. I told her I would love to, and before I could thank her any further she gave me the key and then pointed to a rough white stone on a shelf. "That's my father's only attempt at sculpture," she said. "As you can see, it was not successful." I looked closer: Pound had gouged two eyes into the marble, then crudely carved a vertical line for the nose—but he had cut too deep, and too long, couldn't retract his mistakes, and gave up. Stone, Pound learned, does not forgive impatience.

Mary de Rachewiltz said she had to go, leaving me in a room with billowy curtains. And in that room, as the centerpiece on a round wooden table, stood one of Gaudier's best works, *Boy with a Coney*. I had never seen the work reproduced in color, and so I never knew that the marble had brown veins running like spiderwebs across the two forms: a small figure holding a rabbit with the affection of a Madonna and child. I kept circling slowly to watch how the color of the veins changed when they caught the sun, how the figures themselves moved in and out of abstraction. I tried to imagine myself as Gaudier, standing away from the polished work, and nodding, "Yes, it is done."

That evening, I settled into the cabin and later took a bus into the valley, where I had some dinner. I'd brought my horn along, and when I heard music coming from a bar called Pub One, I walked inside and saw a pianist sipping cognac and playing medleys of swing standards. Couples seated at tables chatted happily. The lights glowed more than they illuminated, and at one point a woman full of giggles grabbed a man's hand, and the two of them seemed to vanish into the back wall. A man in a tuxedo with sleeves too short saw my case and asked if I would play. I nodded. He put his hairy hand on my shoulder and gave me something clear in a crystal tumbler. He kept snapping his head back to let me know this was not meant to be sipped, so I held my breath and knocked it back. The fire began in my throat and then burned straight down through my whole body, and when he refilled my glass, someone else pulled me onto the slightly elevated bandstand.

Who knows what we played, but it was up tempo, and it was fun, and soon people from tables and people from the kitchen crowded the room to dance. During a solo, I heard popping sounds and opened my eyes to glasses of champagne. Someone rolled in a cart with a large wheel of cheese and dark grapes. I drank a good deal of the champagne. Then three waiters rushed in to warn us that the police had arrived. (It was after hours.) About thirty of us crowded behind an enormous curtain against the back wall. Someone kept whispering, sharply, something in Italian that must have translated to, "You crazy sonuvabitch! Shut your mouth!" And then it was over, we spilled back onto the floor, but it was time to leave, and someone drove me home.

In the morning, hungover but still pleased with myself, I stumbled to the de Rachewiltz part of the castle, knocked, and thanked them as best I could. In passing, I mentioned sitting in at Pub One, and Boris's eyes went wide. "Did you hear that, Mary? He played at Pub One!" Now I had a title: I was a musician. They told me the Malinovski daughters and other friends were to arrive that afternoon, and couldn't I stay one more evening to join them all for tea? It would be special, they explained, for it was the night in honor of the Sacred Heart. Throughout the day, people would climb the mountains, as high as they could go, and then, at the top, light bonfires in celebration.

I accepted, of course, and later tried to walk off the alcohol by exploring the land. I passed the vineyards and then, a bit farther, came upon a wooden crucifixion scene within an arbor of scarlet roses. I walked far enough to overlook the stone terrace where Gaudier's *Hieratic Head of Ezra Pound* had grimaced for so many years over the surreal landscape. By four o'clock, I felt ready for tea and conversation, and it was quite pleasant. We all sat outside in a semicircle on top of the castle's main tower. The poet of the gathering read a splendid translation of Dante's canto 8, and then Pound's cousin, who had come with his wife, brought out three recorders. Naturally I must know how to play the recorder, they said, if I could play the saxophone, and gave me the largest of the three. My polite attempt to decline their offer did not work. I was headed for musical disaster, but I did what I could, playing bass lines that swerved into Monk-like accompaniment. Renaissance music never sounded more modern. I apologized, but no one seemed to notice.

Then Mary de Rachewiltz requested that I play some saxophone music—solo. No one had ever done so here, she said, and I really had no choice. Part of me wanted to, anyway. For all I knew, they hated jazz, but it couldn't be any worse than that recorder music, and I left to get my horn. I didn't know what I would play, even as I opened the case in front of their patient, polite smiles. It was now about 7:30, and the snow-covered ranges in the distance warmed to red. I remember the engraved brass of my alto glowing in its case, in my hands. I decided to play the theme to *Black Orpheus* because, for reasons I understood and yet didn't understand, I *had* to. The movie had been an escape from my mother's dreadful deterioration, but the music, like the spiritual nature of this extraordinary visit, brought me back to her.

My eyes closed as the first notes pressed against the darkening air. Two choruses, maybe just one—I don't remember—though I do remember opening my eyes when the final note mingled with the breeze drifting across the stone turret, gently lifting the red-and-white banner draped down the castle wall. All the figures had blended into stone, their applause now silhouetted motion. Around them, and around us everywhere, pinpricks of fire outlined the mountains, orange constellations created by the people who had finally reached their summit and were now burning off the cold, not thinking about the morning when all will vanish to memory, their bodies still warm with a night of flaming hearts and crosses.

# ACKNOWLEDGMENTS

Although this book is dedicated to my children, everyone who knows my family understands that by implication the book is dedicated as well to their mother, the most astonishing person I've ever known.

A number of friends read some or all of these essays, and I'm particularly grateful to Jon Bogle, Thorpe Feidt, and G. W. Hawkes—my older brothers—as well as Gary Giddins, Robin Hemley, Dave Jauss, Patricia Walker, and Bonnie Warwick. Many dear friends supplied specific details, but Lynne Miller provided me with a cassette tape that founded an entire chapter ("Transcriptions"). Carol Martin was not mentioned by name (in "The Wide Hands of Charles Mingus" and "Where We Sleep"), but she strongly encouraged the making of this book, and for her support of my mother before and during her illness, I owe her an incalculable debt. Yusef Komunyakaa brought me to Eastern Washington University Press, where I met Christopher Howell and Pamela MacFarland Holway; the book would not exist without these three magnificent people. Jonathan Johnson offered a number of suggestions that made this a significantly better book; I could not have asked for a more perceptive and generous reader. And I wish Bill Block, Barbara Crawford, Bob Gross, Jim Spenko, my uncle Al, and my father had lived long enough to see this publication; they were, in part, my audience.

Many of these essays were previously published, often in slightly different form: "Black Pearls" (*African American Review*), "Blouse Catching Smoke" (*The New Laurel Review*), "Fire : Ceremony" (*Harpur Palate*), "In Honor of the Sacred Heart" (*Paideuma: A Journal Devoted to Ezra Pound Scholarship*), "Rearview Mirror" (*The Note*), "Spells" (*Hunger Mountain*), "Thelonious Maximus" (*Rivendell*), "Transcriptions" (*Crab Orchard Review*), "Where We Sleep" (*South Dakota Review*), and "The Wide Hands of Charles Mingus" (*Green*

Mountains Review). I'm particularly grateful to *Harpur Palate* and *Hunger Mountain* for nominating the essays for Pushcart prizes.

I would also like to acknowledge a number of sources mentioned in these essays:

Covarrubias, Miguel. *Island of Bali*. New York: Alfred A. Knopf, 1937.

Ellington, Duke, quoted in Nat Shapiro and Nat Hentoff, eds., *Hear Me Talkin' to Ya*. New York: Rinehart, 1955.

Feinstein, Sascha. "Anders and the Norns," "*Coltrane*, Coltrane" (excerpt), and "Summer Cremations" (excerpt). From *Misterioso*. Port Townsend, WA: Copper Canyon Press, 2000. Used by permission of Copper Canyon Press.

Kent, Rockwell. *It's Me, O Lord: The Autobiography of Rockwell Kent*. New York: Dodd, Mead and Company, 1955.

Matthews, Samuel W. "Disaster in Paradise, Part II: Devastated Land and Homeless People." *National Geographic* 124, no. 3 (September 1963).

Matthews, William. "Mingus at The Showplace" (excerpts). From *Search Party: Collected Poems*. Boston: Houghton Mifflin, 2004. Used by permission of the estate of William Matthews.

Melville, Herman. *Moby Dick*. Illustrated by Rockwell Kent. New York: Random House, 1930.

Mingus, Charles. *Beneath the Underdog*. New York: Knopf, 1971.

———. Liner notes. *Mingus at Monterey*. Jazz Workshop JWS 001/002 (1965).

Morton, Margaret. *The Tunnel: The Underground Homeless of New York City*. New Haven, CT: Yale University Press, 1995.

Olsen, William. "The Unicorn Tapestries." From *The Hand of God and a Few Bright Flowers*. Urbana: University of Illinois Press, 1988. Used by permission of the author.

Olson, Charles. "Moonset, Gloucester, December 1, 1957, 1:58 A.M." (excerpt). From *The Collected Poems of Charles Olson: Excluding the Maximus Poems*, ed. George F. Butterick. Berkeley: University of California Press, 1987. Used by permission of the University of California Press.

Pepper, Art, and Laurie Pepper. *Straight Life: The Story of Art Pepper*. New York: Schirmer, 1979.

Rilke, Rainer Maria. "The First Elegy" (excerpt), translated by Stephen Mitchell, copyright © 1982 by Stephen Mitchell. From Rainer Maria Rilke, *Ahead of All Parting: The Selected Poetry and Prose of Rainer Maria Rilke*, translated by Stephen Mitchell. New York: Modern Library, 1995. Used by permission of Random House, Inc.

Spellman, A. B. Liner notes to John Coltrane's *Ascension*. Impulse! Records A(S) 95 (1966).

Williams, William Carlos. "Book V" (excerpt). From *Paterson*, copyright © 1958 by William Carlos Williams. Reprinted by permission of New Directions Publishing Corporation.

The exchange (in "Rearview Mirror") between Howard McGhee and Charlie Parker is based on McGhee's oral account of the incident, as told to Ira Gitler on November 23, 1982. The interview, conducted for the National Endowment for the Arts' Jazz Oral History Project, is available in Carl Woideck's *The Charlie Parker Companion: Six Decades of Commentary* (New York: Schirmer, 1998).